PUTTING THE
GOOD

IN GOODBYE

A Healthy Conversation About the Comings
& Goings of Church People

John Opalewski & Jim Wiegand

Putting the Good in Goodbye: A Healthy Conversation About the Comings and Goings of Church People
ISBN: 978-0-9890546-4-5
Copyright © 2017 by Converge Coaching, LLC
Published by Converge Coaching, LLC, Washington, MI
Email: john@convergecoach.com
Website: www.convergecoach.com

Text & Cover Design: JD Wiegand and Keigh Cox

Acknowledgements

Writing a book is like playing football. Of course, you need players, coaches, and a field on which to play the game. These are the upfront individuals and places you see on television during football season. But football requires more people behind the scenes than it does on the field. Backoffice staff, communications directors, facility and operations managers, technology nerds, legal experts, and scouts, just to name a few. Football games wouldn't happen without an army of people behind the scenes making the product look its best.

God has provided Jim and I with a talented behind-the-scenes team. Here they are:

John:

First of all, thank you to my wife Laura. You are a gift from God, a wonderful partner, and my biggest cheerleader.

A special salute to my sons along with my three daughters-in-law. I love each one you deeply, and with every passing year, value your friendship.

Many thanks to my co-author, Jim Wiegand, for conceptualizing the idea for this book, and your substantial work in its writing. You are an amazing teammate.

Much gratitude to Janet Blakely for your expert editing assistance. You are the manuscript doctor.

Thanks also to JD Wiegand and Keigh Cox for creating a good look to the finished product. Your graphic arts and layout skills are God-send to me.

Many thanks to my Life Group Family. Your prayers, encouragement, and friendship are a lifeline.

Finally, I am grateful to God for the privilege of His call on my life to come alongside leaders and journey through life with them. I get to do what I love for a living, and I owe it all to His mercy and grace.

Jim:

I'd also like to echo John's list from the bottom of my heart. It's an incredible amount of work to write something like this but to be honest, no one would read it without those that make us appear better than we really are.

To Dena my incredible partner in all things for almost 30 years. You're ageless and timeless. Your support and faith in me gives me courage and inspires me to be the man you believe me to be.

My sons (and sons and daughters in the faith), to you I leave these thoughts to help you run the race set before you with wisdom and expectation. Your generation will possess what was only dreamed of in mine. Take the land and possess it for God has surely given it into your hands.

To the wonderful family of faith at The Freedom Center. Your generosity has allowed me to be me for decades as we have served together to build the Kingdom of God and those who would serve in it.

Lastly and most importantly, to the Lover of my soul, Jesus Christ, whose patience, love and wisdom has called me, empowered me and when needed, repaired the broken pieces of my life countless times. Everything good that has ever come out of me came from You my King.

Contents

Foreword

When God called my wife and me into pastoral ministry, we were both excited and scared. We were willing to go anywhere and do anything in obedience to Christ, to see people come to Him and grow to be more like Him. Feeling humbled and blessed to be in ministry, we would have done it for nothing if we could have found a way to feed our family.

As a young pastor I learned that the church was both an organism and an organization. God had given me a heart and vision for the organism—this living body of believers who were called out of the world to make disciples for Christ. The organizational piece existed to make the organism function more effectively. The organization demanded job descriptions, strategic plans, performance reviews, org charts, span of control, measurables, etc.

The general rule in church world is the organization should only exist to support the organism and its biblical purposes. However, conferences and leadership books kept emphasizing the organizational goals including numbers, dollars, growth, percentages, comparisons, top 100, fastest growing, business models. You get it! As a pastor I was continually pulled into the organization with my job description morphing from Shepherd to CEO.

With the difficulty of measuring the organism's growth (love, truth, maturity, stability, etc.), we found it easier to measure organizational metrics.

Don't get me wrong, the organization is important but must be kept in perspective. Christ died for the Church and His Holy Spirit embodies individuals' behaviors as well as the corporate body. When organizational life overshadows the beauty and mission of the church, it begins the death cycle and it's just a matter of time before the church suffocates. The words of Jesus "living but dead" describe this situation.

We as pastors responded to the call to shepherd the church of Christ. While there are many good books on church organizational leadership, I am thankful for John Opalewski and Jim Wiegand's book, *Putting the GOOD in GOODBYE*, that draws us back to our calling, the discipling of people, and leading the Church to be what Christ wants it to be. When people leave the church, pain is inevitable. This book will help leaders process that pain in a healthier way.

The Church is Christ's, and all of us are interim pastors who will one day give an account for the organism. The following pages will prepare you to face that day of reckoning.

Douglas Schmidt
Senior Pastor
Woodside Bible Church

Introduction

"Pastor, I need to talk with you . . ." Those words made me shudder. I feared what was coming next:

"I feel like God is leading us to another church."
"I had a dream . . . and God spoke to me in the dream and told me I'm supposed to leave."
"The glory has departed from this place."
"You don't teach/preach from the King James Bible!"

These actual statements were made to me while a lead pastor many years ago. Each of them preceded a prompt exit from our church. Approximately five years into our tenure as lead pastors, about twenty percent of our attendees had left to find another place to worship.

Just one year before the steady attrition, our church had reached a pinnacle. Record attendance required us to add a second service. More conversions and baptisms happened than in any year prior.

Robust financial giving had swelled the church bank account. Lay leaders stepped up to serve. Momentum was everywhere—then all of a sudden—whammo! Major depression crashed into my life like a burst dam.

While I struggled to work my way back to health, one-by-one, slowly but surely, we began to see an exodus of our members. I took each departure personally, lost sleep, shed tears, got angry, and began to think about a new path for my life. Pastoral ministry had become painful. I felt abandoned, deserted, betrayed, and let down by parishioners who bolted. I joked with my wife about changing the name of our church to Exodus Assembly of God.

Funny thing, graduating with a bachelor's degree in New Testament Biblical Literature didn't prepare me for processing the ebb and flow of people arriving or leaving from our church. I had no understanding of seasons, little appreciation of who these people really belonged to, and what my genuine, God-given role was in their lives.

My lack of preparation and understanding eventually caught up with me. I wanted to leave the position, but with little marketable skills, I felt trapped in the role. I didn't like the feeling of being cornered, but wasn't sure who to talk to or what to do about my dilemma. Two years later I resigned, feeling rather defeated.

When my good friend and colleague Jim Wiegand approached me a few months ago with the idea of co-authoring a book on the subject of processing people's arrivals to and departures from a church, I jumped at the opportunity. No such resource was given to me when I was a lead pastor. And today, very little seems to be written on the topic, even though it impacts every church: large, medium, or small, healthy or unhealthy churches, those in metro areas and churches in rural settings. Every pastor faces the challenges accompanying the comings and goings of people.

I work closely with pastors and ministry leaders today, and I feel their pain as they discuss yet another departure from their church. Jim and I want to help leaders better process their thoughts and feelings when the Christians they've poured their lives into decide to exit.

Our goal in this book is to encourage pastors, give perspective, and provide a game plan or framework for leaders. We hope the real-life experiences, struggles, and lessons learned through pain and disappointment will make your leadership journey easier to navigate. Jim and I want you to be healthy, to love what you do for a living, and to do what you love for a long time.

Maybe you're reading this book while in a season of momentum and growth. We're happy for you. Perhaps you're in a season of discouragement and attrition. We bleed for you. Whichever season you find your church in, the issue of members leaving will never disappear. You can either run for the hills, or learn a better way to think about and respond to the comings and goings of people.

The following pages are written with great passion for pastors and out of the fires of our personal experiences. Jim and I will briefly tell our stories, and then introduce five major ideas related to the comings and goings of the Jesus-followers you pastor. Many ideas could be explored, but we've boiled them down to the five we believe are most critical to understand.

A chapter is dedicated to each one of them. These five are not the only ways to process the "shifting of the sheep." Rather, they serve as a foundation for a healthier approach to deal with the mobility of people in the Church context. Our hope and prayer after reading the pages ahead, is you'll be better positioned to respond to the inevitable flow of attendees in and out of the church you lead.

We are rooting and praying for you!

1 | Jim's Story

In the mid 90s, my wife and I had enjoyed almost ten years of successful youth ministry and had plenty of gas left in our tanks for the next ten. We had the best pastor, the best facility, the best city, and by far the best group of students we ever had the privilege of serving. Every cylinder was firing and every indicator was encouraging.

One day, the lead pastor came into my office and closed the door behind him with a look on his face that I hadn't seen before. It was stone . . . sober . . . serious . . . and a little scary. I quickly reviewed my latest activities to see if I could prepare myself for what he was about to say. Had I done something? Was there a parent I'd spoken to in a way I was about to pay for? We sat and looked at each other for what seemed like an eternity. When he opened his mouth to speak he simply said, "Jim, I wanted you to be the first to know. *We are resigning from the church.*"

Those six words were the beginning of the end of my dreams as a youth pastor. There was no scandal or burnout. It was just time for him to go and he knew it. A year later he was elected to serve as the leader of our fellowship in Arizona where he and his wife have ministered for more than two decades now with incredible success and integrity.

That day began the adventure of a lifetime. I had no idea that the day he walked into my office would start a process that in just a few weeks would lead my young family two thousand miles across the country to enter a whole new phase of life as senior pastors. As we began to search for our next place of ministry, we were full of excitement, dreams, and more than a few fears. With the pastor's help, I polished my resumé and recorded a few messages he allowed me to speak to the adult congregation on Sunday nights. Before long, the phone began to ring and invitations to be interviewed by church boards started coming in.

It was frankly a different experience than any I'd ever had as an associate pastor. Instead of the pastor and perhaps a board member or two, this process was more like a combination of competing in the Miss America Pageant while simultaneously trying to get a Top-Secret security clearance from the C.I.A.

One day as I was sitting in my office, waiting for a call from a pulpit committee, I felt like I needed to take a quick walk and pray. I was nervous and honestly dreading the whole pageant experience once again. As I walked and prayed, I had a strange but wonderful experience. I somehow, without consciously shifting gears, went from praying I wouldn't say anything stupid in an interview, to preaching a wonderful, passionate sermon.

The parking lot I was walking in suddenly transformed into a vast auditorium. The parking spaces became rows filled with people who were listening intently to my instantly broken heart. I preached about a "church" that would care for the lost and hurting, that would live with a constant tension of passion and pain to constrain us and compel us to reach people who didn't know Jesus. Our mission would be to disciple "the found" and send "the ready" to the nations of the earth.

What came out of my heart that day for the first time, is the vision of the church I now serve. That ten minutes of prayer and impartation has been the North Star by which we have navigated our hearts, dollars, hours, and lives for the past twenty-three years.

Ten years of growth

When we arrived in Fenton, Michigan, we had some fairly good cards dealt to us. The facility was outdated, but there was plenty of space. The land had more than enough room to expand in the future. The city was perfect for us! My young family was literally the center of the demographic of those around us. All the dots of our lives suddenly formed a beautiful, clear picture of this place and time. We went to work and after a few tough moments of transition, the church began an incredible ten-year growth track.

In that first decade, we saw the church grow from 99 attendees to more than 1,000. One service became three services. To meet the needs of the congregation coming there were also three separate building projects. It was at this point we began to plant and parent churches. We sent hundreds of people and millions of dollars out to reach others in Fenton, Flint, MI, Georgia, and Mexico. It was our response to what God was doing at the "Mother Ship" in Fenton.

And then it happened

Little by little, as we sent our best and brightest out into the harvest field we began to experience a drain on key leadership positions. After all, you can't send people out who need ministry. You have to send your best. Think of it as a pyramid: the size and stability of its base predetermines the well-balanced height.

Within five years of expansion, we were putting people into important leadership positions who just weren't ready because we hadn't fully prepared them. When a job needs to be done, you have to put the right persons into the position. A wiser man would have slowed the process down but having never been there before, I charged forward as if these emerging leaders didn't need to mature, heal, and grow.

After just a few years of this, the base of our pyramid of leadership was fragile, untested, weak, and in some places, even dangerous. We took note of the number of "problems" coming our way which never seemed to be issues before. We noticed side meetings and subcultures creeping their way into the vision of the church.

What God had given to me that day many years before as I walked around the parking lot of the church had been swallowed up in the human chaos, division, burnout, and fruitlessness of what was now happening. It took a tremendous toll on my soul and the well-being of my family. I was under siege by the preferences and personalities of strong-willed folks. My wife was being attacked by the complaining of attendees who weren't having their "needs" met directly by her in a timely manner. Even our children were fair game for those who looked at them with a critical eye.

After several years, members began to leave the church and

take their circles with them. For one group who left, we weren't "spiritual enough." At the same time, another group exited because we weren't "biblical enough." Others departed because the people who had led them suddenly weren't around anymore.

When those who remained ran into members who left at the local store, and asked why they had left, they were told how leadership had failed them. Then they heard about "The Promised Land" just down the road at another church which was everything our church wasn't. Add to this a few truly twisted folks who used social media several times a day to attack the supposed "heresy" and "lukewarm spirituality." We found ourselves without a moment of peace even with our closest friends who daily assured us they had come to our defense— often publicly scolding our Facebook attackers.

The breaking point

And that's when it happened. I was in Haiti serving the desperately poor human beings who fight day-to-day for their existence with a faith in God that makes me wonder: who's really poor? I

> I closed my laptop and said, "I'm done"

made the mistake of opening my laptop to read a few emails so I wouldn't be overwhelmed when I got back to the "real world." What I found was a quick note from a sweet older couple in our congregation informing me of their intent to leave the church. Apparently, after months of their attempts to get me to change the music more to their liking, I hadn't made enough progress for them to believe it was ever going to be what they wanted.

They also informed me they weren't the only ones who felt this way and others would be following them in the next few weeks.

It was too late for them, but not too late for the others they had spoken to and who had evidently spoken to each other about it at length. When I read the email, I closed my laptop and simply said, "I'm done."

Nothing new

It wasn't the first time I'd felt that way. I'd died a thousand times like most leaders watching their life's work destroyed by churchgoers who'd risked nothing and invested little. But this was the first time the thoughts had made it out of my mouth as heartfelt words. I wasn't angry. I wasn't hurt. I wasn't afraid. I was simply "done." Like someone who finally commits to any action because their hope has died, I was numb, at peace, even nonchalant. It wasn't my conclusion that came out of my mouth. It was what was decided for me. My will to fight had died.

When I came home, I tried to pull it together but there wasn't enough substance left in the broken pieces of my anemic soul to make anything substantial. I eventually told my wife and mentors and then a very few close friends. My leaving became more and more real to me with every conversation with those I left shocked by the revelation. Some tried to encourage me. Others said they didn't know how I'd lasted for so long.

Thank God for my wife Dena

My wife Dena knows me. She seems to know me better than I know myself. Before she would be satisfied with us leaving as the right course of action, she suggested we get away for at least a week to some place where we wouldn't recognize anyone, have any pressure or obligations. God provided just the right place and time.

Phoenix, Arizona is beautiful in February. It's such a change from the often brutal Michigan winters. When we got off the plane, it was an even 100 degrees warmer than when we got on the plane—from minus 20 and overcast, to 80 plus and sunny. We got some sleep—we ate some food—and we exercised in the desert sun. Little by little, a dormant part of me began to wake up.

The event we attended was called the "1,000+ Conference" hosted by Pastor Rob Ketterling. Rob had invited Brian Houston to be the speaker for the small group of leaders gathered there. Little did I know Brian had been through many (and so much more) of the things I was going through at the moment.

God began to speak to me in a way I hadn't experienced in many years. Even the people we sat with at our table for those three days were each God-sent. All were barely hanging on just like I was. All were in pain. All were teetering on the brink of greatness or destruction. In an evening of prayer on the side of a mountain with my wife, God spoke these words to me: "You are the pastor of The Freedom Center."

No sooner had those words permeated my mind when Dena turned to me and said, "So, what is God saying to you?" I reluctantly admitted to her what I had just heard. She looked at me. No, she looked through me and said, "I don't believe you." I asked why and she said, "You're not excited about it. You're always excited about what God says to you."

I repeated to her what I heard God say but also confessed to her I was a little angry with Him for saying it. That may sound strange to you but think of it this way: I was days away from leaving an abusive relationship and that's when God told me to go back to the very thing which had been trying to kill me for the past several years. She hugged me, prayed for me, and took me back to the hotel, and tucked me in.

A new day

The next morning, I woke up around 5:00 a.m. The sun was already coming up. The desert birds were singing. The palm trees were waving hello in the light breeze. As the morning greeted me like a long-lost friend, I decided to go to the hotel restaurant for a cup (honestly, maybe a pot) of coffee.

I opened my Bible and God began to speak to me like I hadn't been able to hear Him speak to me in years. It wasn't anything profound I recall about what the Word was saying to me, it was just speaking to me again. All the voices of dissent, division, and defeat were nowhere to be found. Vision, life, courage, and faith were speaking to me, encouraging me, and exciting me for the first time in a very long time.

After a couple hours of time spent with the Lord, I took some breakfast to my bride. I woke her up with a smile not only on my face, but in my heart. She noticed immediately.

That week was the point of a new beginning for me and the ministry God has called us to. I will never be able to repay Rob, Brian, Dena, and others who were sent to save me from . . . me. The best way to acknowledge their impact on my life is for me to share with others what they taught me during those few days in the desert.

Can you see what happened?

I'm sure after hearing my story, you could help me see the error of my ways, name the mistakes I made, and help guide me away from the dangerous shores I was about to wreck on. But seeing what's wrong after it's wrong is simple. The real questions we need to ask revolve around the thought of how to make sure it never happens again to me—or you.

What did I put in the wrong place? What did I consider priceless that wasn't? What fundamental disciplines did I ignore? What is the truth that can

Ministry is hard!

expand the Kingdom of God without killing the people of God? These are the types of questions John and I hope to help you ask and answer in the next few chapters.

Ministry is hard! It always has been and it always will be, but it's possible to live a well-invested life without losing who you are in the process. It is possible to *mind your congregation without losing your mind*.[1] With this in view, pay careful attention to John's story in the next chapter.

Questions to consider:
1. Think about a time you sped up your life when you should have slowed it down. What factors contributed to your decision?
2. Has God ever led you to a position of leadership you were reluctant to accept? What factors did you work through to move forward confidently in that role?

[1] How to Mind Your Congregation Without Losing Your Mind – Converge Coaching Conference

2 | John's Story

The loud blast of a car horn filled the air . . . dad was waiting for us to pile in the station wagon once again for our weekly trek to church. It was 6:50 a.m. Sunday, and a herd (I have eight siblings) of bleary-eyed kids stumbled into the car for the weekly ritual of Mass. Forty-five minutes of going through the dreaded, mind-numbing motions at church completed my religious duties and I could forget about God until next Sunday.

As a kid I didn't care about God enough to connect faith and behavior. I was a CINO (Christian In Name Only) who played the religious game on Sunday, but lived like the devil the rest of the week. My gutter language, erratic behavior, and mean-spirited treatment of schoolmates was a foreshadowing of even darker days ahead. God grew more distant to me (my fault, not His) with every passing month. Going to church became torture.

As a teenager, I began experimenting with alcohol and other drugs, thinking these would fill the God-shaped vacuum inside of me. "Doping Ope" became my nickname. Yet with the passing of every party, I felt emptier on the inside. I would sit at parties high on pot, people around me laughing and carrying on, while I was feeling desperately alone. On several occasions, I remember staggering across the doorstep to my home and thinking, "there has to be more to life than this."

Enter my friend who lived across the street—Kirk. He had been my friend from age four. We played ping pong, slept over at each other's house, rang door bells and ran away. We "spied" on our neighbors, and generally did anything most goofy teenagers do. We quickly became best friends. Somewhere along the way, Kirk started bringing me to church. His church was totally different than the one I grew up in. I thought some of the people were a bit weird, but they seemed genuinely excited about Jesus.

On June 13, 1974, Kirk invited me to a Christian concert at a local coffeehouse. By this time, I was hip to Kirk's jive. I knew he was trying to convert me to Jesus. But internally I resisted, telling myself: "I'm having too much fun partying my life away." Nothing could have been further from the truth. I was miserable, heading toward a life of drug addiction, and in desperate need of life change. Grudgingly, I agreed to attend—but I remember saying to myself, "I'm not getting converted tonight."

At the end of the loud Christian rock concert, the lead guitar player invited those who weren't Christians yet to follow Jesus. Surprisingly, I found myself wanting to respond. I knew something was wrong with me, something (actually Someone) was missing in my life.

In that holy moment, it seemed as if nobody else was in the room but me and Jesus. He had my attention now, and feeling strangely drawn to Him, I asked Jesus to come into my heart.

Almost immediately, it felt as though a load of bricks had dropped from my shoulders. For the first time in my life, I had this sensation of feeling clean on the inside. Something amazing happened—I felt convinced my old, empty, unhappy life had ended . . . and a brand-new life was given to me.

Many things changed in the weeks to follow. My craving for alcohol and other drugs disappeared. Instead of emptiness, I felt joy, purpose, and a clear sense of direction. My party buddies definitely knew something was different. I shocked them when telling my conversion story. They told me: "You'll be back partying with us in six months." Forty-three years later, I've never looked back.

Within one year of my dramatic conversion, I sensed God calling me to some sort of ministry. I had no idea how to respond to the calling, but sometimes God leads you so clearly, it's not hard to figure out what to do next.

While attending a retreat with my father during my freshman year of college, I met a doctor who just two months prior, had decided to follow Jesus. His conversion was equally dramatic. And as luck would have it, (actually this was a divine appointment), we were assigned seats next to each other for every meal during the retreat weekend. We quickly learned each other's story. The good doctor asked me: "If you could choose any Christian college to attend, which one would it be?" I mentioned Oral Roberts University as my first choice, and then we moved on to another topic.

One week later the doctor invited me and my parents to his house to meet his wife and kids. Halfway into the evening, he pulled me aside, and said eleven words which changed the trajectory of my life: "*John, God told me I'm supposed to send you to*

ORU." I was stunned. My doctor friend, who I had known for all of one week, had just committed to pay for three years of tuition, room, and board.

I applied to the school, was accepted, and trekked to Tulsa Oklahoma for training. I graduated from ORU with a bachelor's degree, and was off to pursue my dream of changing the world for Jesus. I was "ready" to conquer! But lurking in the shadows was a monster I had no idea existed. The spiritual excitement in my life masked an underlying lack of emotional health. Let's fast-forward to November, 1992, when everything changed.

At the time, I was the lead pastor of a growing congregation in mid-Michigan. Life seemed good at home and in the ministry. We were experiencing a banner year at the church. We moved to multiple services on Sunday mornings to accommodate our growing numbers. Men and women were finding Jesus, getting baptized, and growing in faith.

The church's finances were healthy. Everything screamed momentum. But for weeks during autumn 1992, I had trouble sleeping, coupled with no appetite. Seemingly out of nowhere, waves of sadness overwhelmed me, but I had no idea why. Panic attacks and uncontrollable crying spells became common—it was terrifying and I didn't know what was happening to me.

Eventually, living had become so emotionally painful I began thinking about the least painful way to end my life. I put a plan together, and started considering what I would write in my suicide note. My life had spun out of control emotionally.

God in His infinite grace had given me a great wife and wise friends who insisted I see a doctor and a counselor. Both of these men identified the problem. Major depression had brought my world to a crashing halt.

Up to that point, I had no room in my thinking for depression. Depression was something weak people dealt with, not a mature Christian like me. (My arrogance/ignorance was pretty substantial back then.) After all, I had been walking with God for eighteen years. I had been a pastor for twelve years, with measurable ministry growth at every step along the way. My daily routine of Bible study, prayer, and Scripture memory was rock-solid.

Depression colors everything

How could depression happen to someone who loved Jesus as much as me? In that dark moment, I felt betrayed by God. But what I didn't realize then was depression happens to all kinds of people—even to some who love Jesus—even to ministry leaders.

What I didn't understand back in 1992 was the pervasive nature of depression in our world—even in the church world. I somehow overlooked the depressive episodes of King David . . . one of Israel's greatest leaders . . . and the dark seasons experienced by the Old Testament prophets Elijah and Jeremiah, even though I read about them multiple times. I didn't know spiritual giants like Charles Spurgeon, Martin Luther, and John Calvin all suffered from this affliction.

Depression respects no race, social status, gender, or religious persuasion. It afflicts Christians and non-Christians without prejudice—leaders and lay people alike. Depression can happen to anyone. If you have not experienced the long dark tunnel of major depression, let me try to describe what it feels like.

Depression feels like you've plunged into a black hole of sadness

It can engulf you completely, to the point where you feel like an emotional zombie. Listen to the words of an anonymous depression survivor: "When I was depressed and I looked out my window, the landscape looked absolutely flat and colorless." Depression can make a sunny blue-sky day appear gray and gloomy.

In Matthew 26:38, Jesus told His friends in the Garden of Gethsemane, *"My soul is overwhelmed with sorrow to the point of death."* I don't think Jesus was depressed, but His words capture the darkness of depression. When you are depressed, you feel like a dead man walking. Everything and every day feels dark.

Depression doesn't respond to the sheer force of our will

Wouldn't it be nice if you could just will your way out of depression? Or, smile your way out of emotional darkness? Willing or smiling your way to recovery is not possible. You cannot magically snap yourself out of the long dark tunnel. You cannot bargain your way out of depression. I remember frantically negotiating with God while in the middle of the emotional black hole: "Lord, if you get me out of this, I'll do whatever You want me to do." My hope was He would deliver me instantaneously. God had other plans.

Depression often rears up when least expected

In 1992, I had (and still have) a wonderful wife and four healthy boys. I've already mentioned the church I served as pastor was enjoying excellent growth spiritually, numerically, and financially. Externally life was good, but internally I was an emotional train wreck. With depression, two plus two does not equal four.

The professional counselor my wife urged me to see, opened my eyes to understand the truth. And the truth was this emotional crisis that seemingly "came out of nowhere" in November 1992 had been building for years, even decades.

The unique pressures of leading an organization forced to the surface my flawed approach to mental and emotional maturity. My total disregard for sensible scheduling, ignorance of how to handle my anger, and the inability to deal with difficult people finally caught up to me.

This perfect storm thrust me into the battle of my life, hanging on by a thread. My book, *Unshakable You: Five Choices of Emotionally Healthy People (2015)*, addresses in detail how to prevent depression as well as how to recover from its grip.

The unhealthy way I processed people arriving at and leaving from the church added to my distress. Putting the Good in Goodbye addresses a healthier way to think about when parishioners arrive. It also deals with a more mature response when they leave.

In John 10:10, Jesus said, *"I have come that they may have life and have it to the full."* Jim and I are committed to helping leaders live healthy, fulfilling, joy-filled, and fun lives. We believe God intends for His leaders to have fullness in both their personal life as well as their profession. We've written this book out of deep respect for what you do as a leader, and with sincere concern for your long-term health.

We aim to convince you it's possible to lead well and still have a life outside of your ministry, including:

- A great life
- A solid marriage
- Kids who love you and still speak to you
- Time for replenishing friendships
- Regular exercise
- Sufficient sleep

Does this sound like the impossible dream? Rest assured, it's achievable. God wants every pastor to labor in accordance with Matthew 11:29-30: *"Take my yoke upon you and learn from me, for I am gentle and humble in heart, and you will find rest for your souls. For my yoke is easy, and my burden is light."*

Chapter 3 focuses on the foundational rock which will hold you steady as you experience the comings and goings of people. It is the firm footing allowing you to put one foot in front of the other, even in the face of relational headwinds. It is the anchor to keep you stable in the middle of severe people-storms. This rock, firm footing, and anchor centers around your sense of calling. Before moving on to the next chapter, take a moment to think through the questions below.

Questions to consider:
1. Who do you lean on when life punches you in the face?
2. In what ways has God leveraged the painful events of your life?
3. What would have to change in order to have a healthy life outside of your ministry?

3 | What Are You Doing Here?

To be or not to be? That is the question

Legend has it, during the famine brought on by WWII, a young Russian man looked at his life and the prospects ahead of him. Hunger, cold, war, poverty, and hardships were all he could see, and so he began to look for other directions to take his life to a better future.

As he passed a large church, he decided to go inside, say a quick prayer and ask God for direction, but as he walked through the doors, he noticed the incredible art work, the huge ornate fixtures, and just the immensity of it all. That's when it hit him! "I will become a priest," he said to himself. "I won't have to work hard, I will be respected by those around me, I will not be thought a coward, I will never know the cold of winter or the heat of summer and most of all, I will be safe, clean, and well provided for."

Suddenly, an old priest in his robes emerged from a hidden room in the back and stood before him. His beard was long, his hands were clean and without calluses, his clothes were pressed and the more he stood in the presence of the old priest, the more he felt confident of his decision to be "a man of the cloth."

He announced his decision to the old priest and to his surprise, the priest smiled warmly at him, bowed slightly, and motioned for him to follow. Through the hidden door behind the altar they went and then out the back door into the crisp fall air, past the village, and down to the waters of the large river running just on the outskirts.

When they arrived, the priest motioned for the young man to walk with him to the end of a dock protruding out into the frigid water. Although the young man didn't understand why the priest wanted him to do this, he obeyed, believing he was now about to be fully initiated into the priesthood.

When they reached the end of the dock, the priest smiled and for the first time, spoke. "Fully submerge yourself in these waters," he said. The young man hesitated at first and began to question what this old priest might be up to, but the old priest gave him no answers to his questions. He simply waited for the young man to comply with that same kind, warm smile he'd had since they first began just a few minutes ago.

Slowly and with no small amount of pain, the young man and the priest got into the waters. The young man looked to the priest for what was surely about to be his warm congratulations on being initiated into the priesthood, when suddenly, the old priest thrust the young man violently under the water with the force of ten men.

At first the young man thought, this must be some sort of test, but as the seconds dragged on, the burning in his lungs became agonizing and he fought with all his strength until, after some time, he had none left. After what seemed like an eternity, the old priest let him come up for air. That is, the old priest let him come up for a single breath and then, back under the icy waters he went again.

This time the young man knew he was fighting for his life. He began to chop at the hands of the old priest with everything he had but those old, soft hands he had admired just a few minutes prior now seemed made of iron.

Just as everything began to go black, those hands brought him out of the waters and with great force threw him up onto the dock. Slowly, as the lights came back on in his brain, he choked the water out of his lungs and began to take the deepest breaths of his life. It was as if the only thing his body, soul, and spirit could think of was that next desperate gasp of air.

After several minutes had passed the young man gathered enough of his energy to look up and there standing above him was that same warm smile on the face of the man who moments before had tried to kill him. There was only one question that had to be asked as he lay there shivering in the cold. "Why?" "Why did you do that? All I wanted was to become a priest? Why would you treat me like this?!?"

The old priest bent down, placed his arms around the shoulders of the shivering young man as he helped him get into a seated position. He looked into his eyes and this time, for the first time, he wasn't smiling. He looked into the soul of the young man and with the force of a sledgehammer, said these words: "When you want to become a priest as much as you want your next breath, then come back and see me. Until then, *if you can do anything else, go and do it*. You are not called to be a priest."

Right, Wrong or Indifferent

Many reasons explain why men and women engage in vocational ministry. This story helps illustrate what some might be:

It looks easier than what I do for a living now.
It pays well.
People respect spiritual leaders.
The work isn't physically hard.
The people you serve will appreciate you.
The people you lead will love you for it.
God will love you more if you serve Him this way.

By now, if you are in vocational ministry, after reading the list above, you're either laughing or crying! When a person tells me about how he thinks he's called to vocational ministry, I tell him the story of the Russian priest. It may sound like a strange thing to do, to try to talk someone out of the ministry, but in my experience, if I can talk him out of it, he probably wasn't called to begin with.

Has God sent you?

Do you think Moses could have been talked out of his calling after he heard God's voice from the burning bush? Could David have been convinced the prophet was wrong when he poured anointing oil over his head and pronounced him king? Could Paul have found a way out of declaring Jesus and His gospel?

I'm not saying everyone's calling must come from a burning bush, but I am saying although our stories will be different, we all need to *know* we are called to be in vocational ministry—or, we shouldn't attempt it in the first place. Perhaps, if we can do *anything else*, we should.

John: Jim's words above remind me that ministry leadership is not for the faint of heart. The lead pastor role especially, can fulfill and reward you, while it simultaneously squeezes you like a workbench vice. God is working through you, but at the same time, is also working *in* you, pushing up brokenness hidden deep in your heart.

You take relational hits from people which your seminary never talked about, nor prepared you to handle. For some reason, God allows these relationship bombs to drop in your lap. He doesn't allow this because He enjoys seeing you in pain—I suspect it's because He loves you too much to leave you a broken mess. He uses the role to form you on the inside. Unless you have a strong sense of "sent-ness," you'll likely leave before God finishes what He's planned for you and those you lead.

The quiet board member named Peter

Jim: When we came to interview for the church we now serve, at least a dozen men served on the pulpit committee. As a former police officer and student of body language, I sized up the room to see who was impressed, who wasn't, and who needed to be won over. I was doing well with all the men except one. Peter was a Vietnam veteran who looked like Clint Eastwood and although he was polite, he was quiet.

In those two days we spent together, handling hundreds of questions, Peter never asked one. He wasn't detached from the proceedings; he wasn't distant from them at all; he was just quiet and because of that, I couldn't get a feel for him.

As the process was winding down, I decided to ask Peter a question just to get him to talk and see what he was thinking. I said something like, "Peter, you're being quiet. Do you have any questions or concerns we should be talking about? After all, this is a big decision for all of us and no one wants any surprises."

Peter smiled politely and said something I'll never forget. It went something like this: "Pastor Jim, I really only have one question and I've had it since we first started talking to you over the phone a month ago." I leaned in thinking this was going to be a game changer.

He continued, "If you become our pastor, you will be only the second pastor in the 33-year history of this church we all love. Our retiring pastor, his grown sons, and grandsons, as well as their families are planning to stay right here in this church. You are in your 20s; he is in his 70s. Although everyone means well, I believe some really tough times are ahead for the 99 people now attending this church."

Peter finished his mini-speech saying "Any pastor who follows our founder is going to have to live life more as a substitute teacher than a pastor, for what could be years to come. *Frankly, I don't really believe it's possible.* Because of this, I only have one question for you. *Do you believe with all of your heart God is sending you here to pastor this church?*"

I looked him in the eyes and saw a kind man, much like the old priest in the story. He wasn't hoping I'd fail. He wasn't trying to get me to run. He was wise enough to see into an extremely difficult future, and wanted to know I knew God had put me there—or not.

If God wasn't sending me, he knew I wouldn't make it. But if I knew God had sent me there, Peter knew God would get me through whatever was ahead. In essence, he said, "When you want to serve this church like you want your next breath, then come and serve. If you can do anything else, you should do it, you are not our pastor."

From that day to this, I've never hired a staff member without asking this same question. When times grew hard (and they did), Peter would encourage me with my burning bush, my horn of oil, my Damascus Road experience. He'd look me in the eyes and remind me of the promises God made and I was to stand on, as things got harder and harder in the first year. It was moments like that one which gave us what we needed to press on. In some ways, it still is.

Although everything has changed at the church we serve, one thing has remained the same: we stand on a promise, on a commandment from God to serve these people and the world around us. The day we can do *anything* else, we will go and do it because we believe we will no longer be called.

There's only one question

To this day, I think the moment with our board member Peter was a moment sent to us from God. It's a moment I'd like you to have as well. So, let me ask you what Peter asked me over two decades ago:

Do you believe God has sent you to where you are now serving?

There are only three possible answers to this question and no one answer is better than any of the others.

1. "Yes! I know beyond a shadow of a doubt God has sent me to this place for this season." If that's you, then there really isn't much left to say except, hold on to that truth and the God who gave it to you. Remember, you can do "all things through Christ who gives you strength" (Philippians 4:13).

   John: Understanding your "sent-ness" doesn't imply becoming sloppy with your health. Make sure you listen to your body and rest regularly. God gave us the command of Sabbath rest as a gift to protect us from many things, including arrogance. Regular rest reminds us the ministry is God's, not ours. A healthy rhythm of work and rest extends our leadership shelf-life. Now back to Jim.

2. "No." "I think I got here the wrong way, or I'm in the wrong place at the wrong time." No shame exists in anything true. Admit you're in the wrong place, or at the wrong time, and find the right one as quickly as the change can be made. After all, it would be wrong for God to bless you where He didn't send you. Perhaps, in this case your pain is a gift from God to tell you something is wrong and where it's located so changes can be made.

3. "I'm honestly not sure?" Again, nothing is wrong in not knowing, but do you see how important it is for you to know? Jesus said, "Man shall not live by bread alone, but by every word (Rhema) that comes from the mouth of God." We are to live by the promises of the written Word of God (Logos), but we are also to live from the promises God speaks by His Spirit to our spirits (Rhema). It's important that you stand on God's promises. After all, if you don't have a promise, what are you standing on?

Ministry is not a career. It's not simply a set of skills employed to accomplish a goal. It's really like no other life that can be lived. Leading a ministry is an all-out and nonstop honor. (Although, we don't subscribe to the idea you're supposed to be on high alert 24/7).

Pastoring a church can be both terrible and awesome, painful and passionate, sacrificial and fulfilling, beautiful and ugly. And honestly, if you

Ministry is not a career

can do anything other than vocational ministry and have a clean conscience before God, you should do it. Let me go back to our original question at the beginning of this chapter:

"What are you doing here?"

When times get hard and the temptation to quit seems tantalizing, you need to know you are in the right place at the right time with the right stuff. When things are going great, and the temptation to believe you're the reason for the success knocks on the door, you need to know you are in the right place at the right time with the right stuff. When your body says, it can't do one more thing and it's time to rest, you need to know you are in the right place at the right time with the right stuff.

When thoughts cross your mind like: one more board meeting, one more counseling session, needing to raise one more dollar, preach one more sermon, hold one more hand, and hear one more story about who said what to whom—you need to know you are in the right place at the right time with the right stuff.

When you face a world where billions are waiting for the

Gospel and you are only one person, you need to know you are in the right place at the right time with the right stuff.

John: Jim is not calling you to workaholism. He's urging you to understand ministry is hard work. We encourage you to find a healthy rhythm of *work and rest*. Workaholism and laziness are evil twins. Both will destroy you. Health is found somewhere in the middle. To serve in your calling for the long haul, you must locate health.

Jim: This isn't science. No formulas exist for your calling. It's as simple and profound as only relationships can be. It doesn't matter how you know; but it does matter you know you are where you are supposed to be for this season.

To know you are called is to possess the power to never quit. To not know this is to carry a supernatural burden with only your natural strength. The greatest answer to this all-important question is, "I'm doing what God has created me to do and I'm doing it in His timing, by His strength, and for His glory." It is the greatest answer to this question and when you encounter someone who can answer it this way, you will discover they possess a strength few people will ever know.

Now go and ask

I believe the answer to this question is so important that if you don't know you are called to "be a priest" you should take any steps, any time, and at any cost to find the answer. Again, if the answer is "no" or "I don't know," this shouldn't discourage you, it should excite you!

Ask AND it will be given to you.

Seek AND you will find.

Knock AND the door will be opened to you. (Matthew 7:7, emphasis added)

Don't be discouraged if you haven't found the gold mine of your purpose and destiny. Rather, be excited you are in search of the deposit God has hidden FOR you, not FROM you, and He will LEAD you to the greatest treasure of all, a meaningful life, lived for His glory!

Now go . . . and ask
Now go . . . and seek
Now go . . . and knock

If you do know you're called—go! God is with you!

In light of understanding how important it is to be sure you're sent by God, let's get on with the next chapter, and figure out how to put people in their place. When we say putting people in their place, we don't mean giving them a piece of your mind. Instead, we mean assigning them the proper position in God's economy. Before moving on to chapter four, take a moment to work through the following questions.

Questions to consider:
1. How certain are you of God's call on your life?
2. If you're uncertain, who can you talk with to help you figure this out?

4 | Putting People in Their Place

Jim: Somewhere, the American church began to believe a simple but dangerous lie: "The bigger the church, the better, and more successful it is." I'm not suggesting bigger is better or worse. However, the things leaders are willing to do to be "successful" can cause incredible hardships to themselves and those around them, as well as cause the church to become something it was never intended to be. This dangerous thought descends quickly and it looks like this—if bigger is better:

Then the church I lead is a product to be consumed.
The congregation and community are the customers.
Ergo . . .
We must produce what our customer wants if we are to be successful.
If our product isn't enjoyed by our customers, we will soon be out of business.

With two percent of congregations in the U.S. larger than 1,000 people in Sunday morning attendance, and the pastors who lead those congregations being primarily the ones who write the books and speak at the conferences, you can see how this "bigger is better" mindset may become the focus of leaders who serve in vocational ministry. If that's what "success" is, then the leader will feel compelled to do whatever is "working" and "successful."

If you've been a senior pastor for the past few decades like John and I, you will recognize the seasons the church in America has been through trying to be successful. We have been "Purpose Driven," "Simple," "Traditional," "Holy," "Contemporary," "As You Are," and "Everyone is Welcome." We have been "Justice Driven" and "Servant Evangelists." We have followed "The Way of the Master" and "Gone to Where the Fish Swim in the Stream." We have been "Deep Streams" and "Seeker Sensitive."

We have tried everything that worked anywhere for anyone at any time because what we long for is the church to grow. In the end our seating capacity is bigger than ever before, but I fear our sending capacity hasn't kept up with our numerical growth.

One of the greatest dangers you will face as a vocational minister in a local congregation will be a skewed perspective of the people who attend your church. If you see them as the as the embodiment of your success or failure, you are in many ways already doomed to fail even if you "succeed."

The members you serve do have a proper place in your heart, in the church, and in God's Kingdom. Putting them there is paramount to your mental health and the fruitfulness of what God has given you to steward to maturity. Listen to John as he shares just one of his stories.

John: It was a typical Monday morning. Recovering from an exhausting Sunday, I fumbled around in my office, and struggled to be productive. All hope of a quiet day quickly vanished as

George walked into my office unannounced.

George (not his real name), served as a board member and worship leader. He was a generous giver, and an integral part of our church. The look on his face foreshadowed bad news—and his words confirmed it: "John, we're leaving the church. We don't feel like we're being challenged enough, so we're going somewhere else."

I was shell-shocked. George was well-respected within the church, and for good reason. He was a gem—the kind of guy you want to clone and build the church on. Losing him (and his family) was a painful punch in the gut. George's kids were my kids' friends. George's wife was my wife Laura's friend. This one hurt instantly. I mumbled to him: "Okay, George, if that's what you feel you need to do . . ."

As soon as he left the office, rapid-fire questions bombarded my brain. "How are we going to replace George?" "Will other people leave because he's leaving?" "How will we make it up financially?" "What will this do to my leadership?" "God, are You trying to kill me?" Catastrophic thinking hit high gear. Here's what I didn't understand at that particularly frustrating moment: From a leadership and stewardship perspective, *I'd put George in the wrong place.*

Today, as I reflect on his departure, along with others who had exited, I realize my understanding of people's place in God's economy was flawed. I operated as though once a person got plugged into our church, it was a life sentence. Subconsciously, (I'm so embarrassed to admit this), I thought they belonged to me. In my mind, we were joined at the hip, and any exit by them felt like a betraying slap in the face. My inaccurate and immature perspective increased the pain level when friends I had poured time and energy into decided to bolt for another church.

So, what is the proper place for people like George? What's a better way to view the families who attend your church? What approach will keep you more even-keeled emotionally when brothers and sisters in Christ head for "greener pastures"? How do you put people in their proper place? Here it is:

God's people are His people, not yours

Pause for a moment and reflect on those words. *God's people are His people, not yours.* They belong to Him, not you. I understand the reluctance some pastors might have accepting this idea. They may insist: "If there's a good chance folks will leave sometime in the future, why should I pour my life into theirs?" Good question. I get it—you want to invest in men and women who will be around for a long time, and who will help achieve the mission.

> **God's people are his people, not yours** A reaction of this nature makes perfect sense. But I wonder if it makes sense to God. I wonder if we have to get our minds off our corner of the vineyard, and get them wrapped around the larger, macro picture of God's kingdom.

The people in the church we serve are not our people and never will be. They belong to God! So, *we pour into them because that's what kingdom-minded leaders do.* We're called to build *the* kingdom, not *our* kingdom.

I like baseball, but I don't always understand baseball. The sport comes with a boatload of unwritten rules. Here's a frightening one: If the opposing team's pitcher plunks one of your teammates with a 98 m.p.h. fastball, your pitcher is obliged to bean one of their teammates with the baseball at a later point in the game.

Hockey has similar unwritten rules. If a large defenseman from the opposing team roughs up your star center, your toughest teammate drops the gloves later in the game to "set things in order."

The Church is full of unwritten rules as well. One is: Once a person says, "I'm in," they're *in—forever.*" Could this unwritten rule, dancing in the subconscious minds of pastors, be multiplying our pain when members leave?

> **We're called to build *the* kingdom, not *our* kingdom**

Instead of relating to your people as lifelong, long-haul attendees who by some unspoken rule are obliged to be with you until the grave, perhaps it's healthier to think of them as seasonal. Maybe approaching the relationship with the understanding that you likely will have them for a limited amount of time, will make their departure easier to accept.

The question isn't, how long will (or should) they stay—the question is, how will you steward the time you *do* have with them? In what specific ways will you make the most of the opportunity?

It's tempting to devolve into a beggar in departure scenarios, to grovel, "I'll change, the atmosphere will change. I'll start preaching better! We'll turn the music volume down! We'll even change direction if you'll just stay!" We, in effect, bargain with people and in doing so, set ourselves up for future trouble.

Changing the core of who we are in a desperate attempt to keep people longer than we should is a recipe for crazy. Our identity will blur. We'll give people power over our happiness and sense of value.

We cannot be owned by God and people simultaneously. If we're owned by people, we'll live by their praise, die by their criticism, and ultimately be crushed by their departure. Obviously, all three results are unhealthy. In the end, your identity as a loved child of Father God will slide toward an identity swallowed up by what you do for a living.

> **Work *from* your identity, not *for* your identity**

The more you learn to work *from* your identity instead of *for* your identity, the better prepared you'll be to process the arrival and departure of people. Perhaps you need a come-to-Jesus-moment to help you grasp one of the most important lessons a leader will ever grasp: *your ministry is not your identity—your identity is rooted in an unshakable relationship with Jesus Christ.*

Leading from your identity will temper your enthusiasm when attendees arrive, and lessen the sting when those you've discipled decide to move on. Proper identity frees you to remain true to how God has created you, to be the best version of yourself you possibly can, and to become confident enough to let the relational chips fall where they may.

At the time of a steady exodus of parishioners away from the church where we were lead pastors, I worried about what the denominational leaders would think of our attendance decline. Would their opinion of me be irreparably damaged? Would they look at me through the lens of the decline? Would it become the lasting image in their minds? No denominational leader ever said anything negative to me about our struggles, but I was over-the-top (and needlessly) fearful they did behind closed doors.

What about my pastoral colleagues? Due to our steady attendance decline, I dreaded regional events where they would pop the inevitable question: "How many are you running?" I wonder how many leaders avoid these gatherings due to fear of answering that dreaded query.

My obsession with numbers was a large contributor to the angst felt when the next couple called me and said: "Pastor, we love you, but . . ." Jim and I are not suggesting numbers are insignificant. Healthy organizations grow. Numerical goals are not inherently evil. They can produce focus. They tend to bring order to your week. Numbers can be useful measuring sticks for charting progress. The question is, which numbers matter the most?

The big change for me now as opposed to thirty years ago? Different numbers matter. Don't misunderstand—attendance is important as an indicator, but it's probably not the best or most reliable indicator in the 21st century. In the 1980s and 90s, attendance was the key performance benchmark for most churches. A big crowd was considered undeniable proof of organizational health.

But given today's rollercoaster attendance patterns, Sunday morning numbers seem a less reliable barometer. The number of members attending small groups might be a better indicator of health. Service engagement can be a more dependable measuring stick. What I mean by that is the number of attendees who call your church "home," and serve inside or outside the church. The percentage of people released into their God-given gift and passion areas is probably a better gauge of overall health.

At one church where I recently served as associate pastor, 85% of our adults and students engage in some form of service either at the church and/or outside the church. While I think 85% is healthy, I believe we could do better. We observed an unexpected pattern: The more members were involved in leading a team or working on a team, the more our attendance stabilized.

Other non-number-centric indicators of organizational health include trust, clarity, and communication. Does the leadership team trust one another enough to be vulnerable with each other? Can they admit weakness? Mistakes? Does the church have a clear vision of its future destination, along with a deadline for arriving there? How far down into the organization does this picture live? Are people and resources aligned around the destination? These indicators reveal health—or lack of health, depending on the answers to the above questions.

Fixating on Sunday morning numbers becomes dangerous when it becomes a leader's sole focus. We walk on thin leadership ice when our sense of value rises and falls on the weekly attendance sheet. We put our character at risk when we feel or act superior to our pastoral peers because more people stroll through our doors than theirs. God forgive us for such blatant and arrogant sin.

Numbers become dangerous when we treat attendance as the primary indicator of progress instead of only one of many indicators. Attendance doesn't capture the full picture of organizational health. Announce free pizza for next Sunday's service, and you'll have a big crowd—but it doesn't mean you're healthy.

We're not promoting the goofy idea of growth being meaningless. Healthy things grow. Pastors who loudly insist: "Growth doesn't matter" tend to be leading non-growing churches. Here's what we *are* promoting: God sent you to your current post to be found *in* Him . . . for them. (Pause here and ponder the previous statement.) God didn't send you to be found *in them* . . . for Him. Remember your true identity isn't what you do for a living—it's Who you belong to—Father God.

How do we put people in their proper place? By reminding ourselves every day they belong to God, not us. By understanding our relationship with Father God is our identity and source of value instead of our ministry. By believing He doesn't love us more when our church grows, or less when it doesn't. Ephesians 1:5 states: "In love He predestined us to be adopted as His sons through Jesus Christ, in accordance with His will and pleasure." Paul links our identity to adoption as sons into Father God's family.

We put churchgoers in their proper place when we discover

our true self is found in Him, not in our calling. *We're not pastors first who happen to love God. We're lovers of God first who happen to pastor.* Grabbing on to our real identity will keep us whole, and keep our congregation properly positioned in our head.

Before you move on to chapter five, tell yourself out loud: "God's people are His people, not mine." Perhaps rehearsing those words every morning would benefit you.

But understand: It's one thing to put God's people in their proper place intellectually. It's an important milestone to think this way—but your work is not finished. You must learn *how* to lead accordingly.

The rubber meets the road when people arrive at your church's doorstep. The next chapter outlines how to behave toward people when they first show up. Before you jump into chapter five, take a moment to reflect on the questions below.

Questions to consider:
1. What are a few practical ways you can put God's people in their proper place?
2. What measurements are you using today to determine the health of your church?
3. Which measurements do you need to add? Subtract?

5 | When People Arrive

A healthier way to say "Goodbye" starts with a healthier way of saying "Hello."

Jim: As a vocational minister, only you know the sacrifices, the effort, the real costs of doing what you do. You also know the rewards. Few things are more rewarding to me than when a new person or family looks me in the eyes and says, "We have decided to become part of what God is doing here." In that moment, the costs fade and pastoring becomes so worth it. They get it! They see what I see! I'm not crazy! They value what I'm pouring my life into and they are going to share this burden, this dream, and this life with me!

I can't imagine what it must have been like on the Day of Pentecost, when thousands gave their lives to Jesus and were baptized both in water and into the Apostolic dream that was the Church. After everything the disciples had been through with Jesus and those who hated him, now, in that moment, it all must have made sense.

It may seem like not much needs to be said about the good times. After all, who needs help once the dream comes to pass? But that's the danger of arriving. In ministry, there will always be another mountain to climb, another soul to save, another mouth to feed, and another person who needs ministry.

People may arrive, but we don't

The best way for me to describe what I mean comes from an excerpt in my book, *"Why" is Greater than "What."*

One thousand miles south of San Diego, in the middle of the Baja Peninsula of Mexico, is a town most people have never heard of, where I found myself a wedding guest of people whom I had just met. We were on a trip to find new places where we could help people who lived in the scorching heat, and where gut-wrenching poverty plagued the area at the time.

A young couple invited us to attend their wedding—what an honor bestowed on complete strangers. With the promise of fresh goat meat, homemade tortillas, and new friends, we agreed to stay an extra day in the area and enjoy this village full of smiling faces. After the wedding came the reception and, as honored guests, we sat next to the local pastor who performed the ceremony. A conversation ensued that changed my life. Not only that, it was the beginning of a whole new way to look at my life and the lives of those around me.

The Most Successful Failure I Have Ever Met

As polite conversation with this pastor gave way to more intimate topics, I discovered in this remote village, the church he served had approximately three hundred members who were a regular part of the fellowship. I was shocked there were even three hundred people in the area! As harsh of an environment as it was, how could it meet the needs of the local farmers and herders?

When he saw I was impressed by the size of his congregation, he looked down at his food as if he were uncomfortable with the topic. In an attempt to relieve the tension I had created for this humble man, I made what I thought was an appropriate comment. I intended it to be the final word on the subject so we could move on, and said to him, "Wow! Every person in this area must be a believer in Jesus."

It has been my experience in cross-cultural settings that I unintentionally say the wrong thing, only to have the host gently correct me. But this time was different. The man looked as if he was going to cry. He politely excused himself from the table of honor and left the adobe building, going out into the brutal desert heat. I knew I had said or done something wrong—something which was perhaps inexcusable.

After what seemed like a long time, I decided to approach him and apologize for whatever I said or did to cause such a reaction. I found him outside in the only sliver of shade available at the back of the building. He was alone and in tears. When he saw me coming, he wiped his face with his hands and tried to pull himself together, embarrassed by his emotions. When I began my apology, he stopped me and accepted responsibility for what he was experiencing.

This was his explanation: "Brother, when you were impressed by the size of my congregation, it was humbling because I know the amazing things God has done for these people. I deserve very little credit for all that has been done. I am like the donkey Jesus rode into Jerusalem who has the honor of carrying Him through my village so by lifting Him up, others can see who

He is. But when you said you thought every person in this area must be a believer in Jesus, it was more than I could bear. You see, everyone is not yet a believer. *There are still two that do not believe.*"

After he said that, he could no longer control his emotions; he began to weep like a father weeps for his wayward children. I stood there in silence as this holy moment played out before my eyes. If this man had been in the ministry for self-promotion, he would have been writing blogs and books about how to get 99 percent of your community to come to church every Sunday, but that wasn't why he was living this life of service.

He had found his purpose and it was not only changing the world around him, *it had also changed him.* As the sound of his broken heart for two lost sheep filled my ears, I felt a great compassion for him. My desire to partner with him and see his precious two lost sheep come to faith was cemented into my soul.

From this story, I want to extract several truths for us to consider when people arrive.

Humility

The fastest way (in my personal experience), to see God's blessings leave what I'm doing is to take credit for what *He's* doing. A blessed AND humble leader is one of greatest balancing acts in the world. When everything is going wrong and people are leaving, no one needs to remind me to stay humble. But when God is blessing in visible and tangible ways, it is tempting to believe I am the "secret sauce" to that blessing.

I have no doubt God has given you incredible gifts, abilities, and talents. You, my friend, are a walking miracle of grace on display for all to see. However, the minute you decide to claim the credit for the "gifts" on loan from God, you will suffer the fruit of such a mistake.

John: The apostle Paul wrote: "I planted the seed, Apollos watered it, but God made it grow. So, neither he who plants nor he who waters is anything, but only God, who makes things grow" (1 Corinthians 3:6-7). The most accomplished missionary in the history of Christianity, and the most prolific writer of the New Testament, never forgot where his success ultimately came from. His mantra? *All I did was plant—God made it grow.*

When our church gets bigger, human nature draws us to a place of misplaced credit—and the more we yield to this nasty part of our flesh, the more our
head swells with pride. *Everything good in our ministries comes from the gracious hand of God.* He's given us the ability, the personality, the open doors, and the opportunity to succeed. Yes—we have a part to play—planting and watering. But God is the one who brings the growth.

God brings the growth

I (Jim) like what the humble pastor in Mexico said, "I am like the donkey Jesus rode into Jerusalem who has the honor of carrying Him through my village so by lifting Him up, others can see who *He* is." This is truly a brilliant analogy. Of all the things Jesus could have used to be clearly seen by the crowds that day, He hand-picked a donkey colt, an animal who *felt* unqualified, inexperienced, and probably scared, who had no idea what was actually going on.

It's an honor to be used by Jesus to lift Him up for all to see. How silly it would be for the animal to think the crowd praising Jesus was actually praising him. It would be like the donkey walking along hearing the people and gradually thinking, "I must be important. I must be special. These people really love me." It won't be long before the same colt would start thinking, "I wish this guy would get off my back. He's kind of cramping my style."

Gratitude

A better way for the donkey colt to look at the scenario is to say, "WOW, I can't believe I get the honor of being a small part of what Jesus is doing in this city, in this moment, in His Kingdom."

Growing up, I was always the fat kid with the glasses—picked last in kickball, picked last in dodgeball—picked last in anything including a ball, a stick, running, throwing, jumping or strength. Add to this my challenge of not caring about academic things and after a while, you'll see when it came to stuff that gives a kid self-esteem, I didn't have much going for me.

I am God's favorite kid! When Jesus picked me to play on His team, I couldn't believe it! Not only did He choose me but He gave me abilities to communicate. This was noticed by my teachers, but not encouraged because it usually happened at the same time they were talking.

Through the years, doors opened to speak in prisons, churches, school assemblies, to business leaders and military personnel.

Each time I was able to connect with others and be a small part of some rather huge things He was/is doing. You have to believe me when I say, I am God's favorite kid! There is no other explanation for His kindness to me.

I labor with this firm conviction: I do not make sense anywhere else except in God's Kingdom. Before you think I'm delusional, I'd invite you to join me in this belief. I believe we are all God's favorite kids, and He has given gifts to all of us which make us all incredible. If you believe this, you have no other option but to use those gifts loudly for His glory with great gratitude in your heart.

When people arrive at your church and connect, always remember the honor God has given you in being a small part of His huge story in their important lives, and be thankful to serve both God and them. Your job is to gratefully lift Jesus up high enough so He stands out in the crowd and can be clearly seen by those who pass by.

Broken

It takes a special heart to reach so many and still hurt for the few. In Luke 15, Jesus tells three parables revealing his heart for those who don't yet know Him: The Lost Sheep, The Lost Coin, and The Prodigal Son. Each time, Jesus shows us a glimpse of God's broken heart for those He loves and the incredible value He places on "the one."

This God-given pain for the lost is a beautiful gift which keeps those who will bear it from going the wrong direction in ministry. Think of it this way: I am a parent of two sons. If the house they were in was on fire, everything in me would focus on where they were and what I needed to do to get them out of there before the flames consumed them.

If, after some time, through the smoke, I saw the outline of one of them escaping and I ran to him and threw my arms around him, what two questions would I ask? If you're a parent of two children, you know the answer to this question. The first one will sound something like, "Are you OK? Are you hurt? Did you get burned? Can you breathe?"

Once I hear the answer to the first question, I will immediately ask the second one. Can you guess what it will be? Remember, I have two sons. I am weeping tears of gratitude because this one is safe! But, I have two sons. I'm bursting at the seams because this one is in my arms! But I have two sons. The second question I'm going to ask my first son is, "Do you know where your brother is? Is he OK? Do you know how I can get him free from those flames?"

When you love the lost and value them the way God does you will escape the two biggest traps waiting for everyone when people arrive at their front door. The first trap is to feel successful and satisfied. If your heart remains broken for people, you will never be satisfied even though 300 of the 302 people in your area attend the church you pastor.

How could any parent approach the burning building with their kids in it and say, "Well, one out of two ain't bad?" The second trap is to quit. Believe it or not, a growing church, even a healthy one, takes an incredible toll on those who serve it. The work is endless and can suck the life out of your soul, tax your family, and exhaust you in just a matter of a few *good* weeks.

When you are in pain for those who do not yet believe, there is a much better chance you will stick to what you've been called to do even when it gets painful. *Or better yet, you'll learn how to rescue them without destroying yourself in the process.* What parent could quit trying to rescue their child from a burning building because it got hard? What parent wouldn't want to rescue as many as possible by staying healthy and ready when the time comes?

John: Many years ago, my seventh-grade teacher Mrs. Anderson, screamed at me during math class: "Shut up John! All you do is talk-talk-talk!" Like Jim, I loved to talk, and usually in unison with Mrs. Anderson. I wonder if my frazzled teacher would get a kick out of what I do now: *I listen and talk for a living.* I listen to and talk with pastors, ministry leaders, missionaries, business leaders, etc. I love every minute of what I do. The thought, "God, I can't believe I get to do this kind of work," crosses my mind every week, especially after a mentor session with a pastor or a consulting meeting with a leadership team.

I have the distinct privilege to walk alongside great leaders during their times of personal and professional adversity, and to rejoice with them during moments of achievement. I have a front-row seat to their problems, pressure, and progress—and even get paid for the pleasure of journeying with them. I work behind the scenes so they can shine on the public stage. Who wouldn't love this kind of work?

But here's the rub: they don't stay my clients forever. Our professional relationships have a shelf-life. When they arrive for mentoring or consulting, we go in knowing the arrangement is for a season. In those moments, it's clear I'm merely one link in a long chain of movement toward their full potential. It's humbling to be used as an instrument of God in their journey—and humbling to be reminded I'm only one of many instruments God will use to help them grow.

When they move on, obviously some sadness emerges. I miss our regular talks. They've become my friends. The good news is, even after our work together has finished, we remain friends. I don't feel slighted because they move on, even when it's to another mentor or consultant. I still pray for them regularly. At regional or statewide events, we eat together, laugh together, and enjoy each other's company. They are God's guys—not mine. I'm learning to hold them loosely.

God's people are His people, not yours. When they arrive, remember to be humble, grateful, and broken. Always keep in front of you this: you are but a link—an important link—in a long chain of God's work in their lives. This approach sets you up to better handle the part of pastoring every pastor deals with—when they say goodbye.

One final note regarding the arrival of new people to the church. When newcomers arrive at my home church, we allow no bashing of the former pastor. If their previous pastor was truly toxic, and the new arrival cannot resolve the pain on their own, we encourage them to see a counselor to help scrub out their wounds. Avoid getting tangled in the trap of listening to a negative verbal barrage about the new arrival's former leader.

The intent of this chapter was to alert you to new ways of thinking about and processing the comings of people. In the next chapter, we'll consider a new approach (well, maybe new for most of us), to processing the goings of people from our church. Take a minute to answer the questions below before diving into chapter six.

Questions to consider:
1. Consider your typical response to the arrival of people at your church. What parts of your response need adjusting?
2. How can you consistently right-size the view of your role in the lives of those who decide to attend your church?

6 | When People Go

When people leave your church, God often mourns—and so should you—at least for a while. No words we can write will totally erase the pain of a member's departure. Our hope is a proper perspective on the leader's part will reduce the hurt felt when a friend says goodbye.

Let me (John) give you a real-life illustration from one of my roles in the marketplace. "Oscar, I can't keep you on the team. I have to let you go." Oscar (not his real name), sat in stunned silence as the words no employee wants to hear sunk in. As I outlined next steps, he mumbled in response: "I understand. I don't like it—I'm mad at you—but I understand." Oscar wasn't leaving at his choosing. He was leaving at mine.

You can imagine the tension gripping the room. (The anxiety building up to these types of conversations tends to be worse than the actual conversation.) I did everything in my power to give him a soft landing with a compassionate severance package. I sincerely thanked him for all the good things he'd done for our team and the technology company we served.

I tried to handle this difficult conversation with grace. I didn't want to crush the guy—I honestly wanted the best for him. I went out of my way to avoid burning relational bridges with Oscar. Yet at the end, I still felt sad.

The IT world is small in many ways, and wouldn't you know it—three years later Oscar and I ended up working together on the *same team* at another technology company. Because our parting, years earlier, was doused in grace and concern, we had no baggage to work through relationally. For both of us, there were no personal walls to scale. We ended up working well together, and even sharing laughs with each other.

I understand when people leave a church it's usually their decision, not ours. But the same principle applies. How do we bless them when *they* choose to leave? How do we allow for a graceful exit? How do we avoid burning relational bridges or erecting walls so in the future, they can come back to our church without having to overcome a departure made ugly by our lack of grace?

The art of blessing people when they leave is exactly that—an art. Sure, best practices exist, but every departure is unique, and requires somewhat of a custom approach. Pastors wrestle with these questions: How will this *hasta la vista* impact the church? Who else will leave on this person's coattails? How much information should I share and with whom? What will this do to our finances? What if those who remain are told a pack of lies about the circumstances surrounding this person's exit?

Most of your congregation will never know the real story behind someone leaving your church. Their view will tilt on what they hear from the departed member, or even worse, by what they read on social media.

It's incredibly tempting as a leader to set the record straight, to defend yourself, to point out how right you are and how wrong the person is who's leaving. But my experience tells me *defending yourself in this manner isn't the best strategy.* In my book, *Unshakable You: Five Choices of Emotionally Healthy People,* I share appropriate times to defend yourself. When members depart, we may create more turbulence when we react defensively. We might make matters worse when we try to clear the air with the entire congregation.

Pastoral ministry is deeply personal

So, what's a leader to do? Running away screaming may enter your mind. Curling up in the fetal position under your desk may seem reasonable. Seriously though, how do we learn and then operate in the art of blessing people when they leave?

Understand it's sometimes right for people to leave

Perhaps God sent an "Oscar" to you for a season, to teach him something he could best learn from you, to bring healing to a broken area of his life, or to launch him into the next phase of his God-given purpose. Or maybe, God sent him to you so Oscar could teach *you* something, or help bring healing to a broken part of *your* life. Either way, there is a time and a season for everything (where have we heard that before?)

Legitimate reasons to leave a church exist. Leadership abuse and heretical teaching top the list. Occasionally, God honestly calls a person to help at another church. However, most churchgoers who bolt don't do it because of abuse, or heresy, or God's calling.

Sometimes people leave due to systemic issues within the church. Perhaps the general leadership style is heavy-handed, authoritarian, and dismissive of others. Maybe the church's pace is so fast members get burned out and decide to find a congregation with a healthier approach to scheduling. Departures can be an opportunity for leaders to look in the mirror, and ask: Am I contributing in any way to their departure?

Multiple visions under one roof equals division

A while back, I asked a person at a church we were consulting with: "What's the vision of the church?" His answer: "The pastor's vision, or my vision?" Yikes. Our awkward exchange reminded me that sometimes a person leaves because of vision problems. A member who can't buy into the vision of their church, or wants to actively promote a different vision, *needs* to say goodbye and find a church with a more compatible vision.

Multiple visions under one roof equals division. Unfortunately, most departures don't fit under reasonable categories. Most of the time, it's either an issue of control or consumerism. Consumerism is demonstrated when people hop from church to church in a quest for a place that will meet or exceed all of their expectations. Consumerism is characterized by shallow commitment and selfishness.

As I've grown over the years, certain relationships have been added, and others have been pruned away. Not all of the pruned away relationships were necessarily bad relationships. It's fascinating to read Jesus' words about God the Father in the Gospel of John: "... every branch that does bear fruit He prunes so that it will be even more fruitful" (John 15:2).

Our Heavenly Father doesn't only prune unfruitful branches, He also prunes those already bearing fruit. Why? Because He wants more growth.

All of us have had to say goodbye to certain friendships (can you say high school?) to make room for healthier ones. Some of our relationships are seasonal. I can think of several friends from the past who are not in my life anymore. Not because bad things happened, but because God put them there for a limited amount of time. I wonder if this has application in the church setting? Is it possible God is behind some departures?

Understanding it's healthy in certain circumstances for people to leave helps us right-size our expectations and reduce (not eliminate) the pain associated with their departure. This leads us to the next point.

Grieve

When people I discipled left our church, I was shocked. Then I got angry—angry at them for leaving, and angry at myself for not preventing it from happening. Then I got sad. I was unknowingly walking through several stages of grief—shock, anger, and sadness.

It's appropriate and healthy to mourn the loss of people, especially those you've poured time and energy into. It begs the following questions: Why am I feeling disappointed and angry when those I've discipled leave? What unhealthy expectations did I have of them from the beginning? Am I struggling with who they really belong to?

Fortunately, or unfortunately, pastoral ministry is deeply personal. Most ministers throw themselves into their work with energy, optimism, and love for those they lead. When people abandon ship for illegitimate reasons, it's difficult not to take such actions personally.

However, my sense is a leader's mourning is not to be long-term. Rather, we need to grieve for a season—and then move on. Grieving is part of the healing process, so don't try to go around it—you need to go through it—just don't get stuck in your grief forever. Get back to focusing on the good things happening in your church. Vigorously celebrate wins. Give profuse thanks for those still on board with you. Devote time to your biggest opportunities. Get back on the horse and ride. Stay on mission.

A shared burden is automatically cut in half

I'm also thinking ours is not to be a public mourning . . . in the sense we grieve openly in front of the entire congregation. Sharing our grief with God is a good start. He's already grieving with you. If anybody understands what it feels like when people jump ship—God does. He can relate to our pain. Pouring out our feelings to Him is both wise and therapeutic. He gets it, and can help.

Sharing our grief with a select group of people—our spouse, a trusted mentor, our board—is healthy. Stick to the facts, ask for prayer, and remind them to maintain confidentiality. A shared burden is automatically cut in half, so avoid the quicksand of trying to walk through loss alone.

Say goodbye graciously

Last summer I met the pastor of a large church in the Midwest who, believe it or not, eats cake with those who decide to leave. He chooses the kind of cake—but nonetheless, they actually consume cake together. It's his unique way of blessing people on their way out. Nothing is to be gained by vengeful goodbyes. Everything inside of you may be screaming "let the jerk have it."

Caving in to the urge to blast away may feel good in the moment, but it doesn't take a genius to figure out the pleasure will be short-lived, and not worth the long-term damage. Giving in to your anger at this moment will burn bridges and reduce the possibility the target of your rage will ever return. And you'll diminish your leadership credibility with those members who remain.

Be gracious when people leave. Thank them for their contributions (if any) to the progress of the church. Wish them the best for their future. Commit to them you'll never throw them under the bus—and ask them to extend you the same courtesy. If it's true, tell them you will miss working together.

Jim: More than twenty years ago, when we first came to the church we now pastor, we were young and had little experience with adult people saying goodbye. As youth pastors, we knew from the beginning we only had a few years to make an impact before our kids would be out into the adult world. Because of that, we led with our absence in mind. Let that sink in for a moment.

We, like Jesus, knew the time we had with our kids was a limited engagement and after we were done in their lives and they moved on, all that would remain were the lessons they had learned *and* could apply. This mindset is a good one for those who lead adults as well. When we create environments requiring our people to be "our people" to succeed, we set them (and our organizations) up for failure.

> *One of the greatest mistakes we can make is to consciously or subconsciously create a culture that celebrates when people are retained instead of released*

Remember, the five-fold ministry gifts are to prepare "God's people for works of service." If your heart is to serve God and people as a leader, you must embrace from your heart the moments when your third-graders graduate to fourth grade. Bigger isn't always better. Retaining folks you are supposed to serve for a season, and then vilifying them for graduating is a terrible use of your God-given authority.

I know it's hard to grasp, but the reality of pastoring in our culture remains—your time in their lives is probably for a season. If we concentrate on making the season what God wants it to be, then we will succeed.

Some will stay and serve as pillars in your church, but some will leave for other things, other places, or other leaders. Like it or not, it's a reality you must accept or you will suffer for no reason. You will give Satan a foothold in your heart for no reason. You will withdraw from people God sent you to for no reason and worst of all, you will look into the face of your success and label it a failure.

God is measuring your ministry. His two measurements have

nothing to do with who stays and who goes. *Quality and fidelity matter to God.* "Well done, good and faithful servant!" (Matthew 25:21), is the moment we are to live for. "Well done" is our quality and "good and faithful servant" speaks of fidelity. Do the best you can to feed the sheep and set captives free. You are a servant to all but you only have one Master. In the end, who stays and who goes isn't up to you. It's up to the people and their God.

Quality and fidelity matter to God

Let those who are to go, go graciously, even if it gives you a temporary heartache or even a black eye. People aren't stupid. They'll see what's done in secret eventually. Wisdom is proved right by her actions. Making the people who leave look like villains (even when they are) makes a toxic environment of fear and redefines in an unhealthy way what loyalty means.

When we create a culture celebrating graduation, sending, and next steps, people actually want to stay as long as they can. *When we make villains out of those who leave, people still leave, but they leave having to justify their actions.* After all, if leaving is evil, then those who leave must make what they are leaving more evil.

I hope you're getting this. When your pain at their leaving causes you to react badly, it doesn't prevent people from leaving, it only makes their leaving more problematic for them, you, and the church.

Lead with an open hand to those who walk in and walk out of your church and you will stay emotionally healthy and heal many wounds. Lead with a closed fist and you will continually fight a battle you can't win, and suffer through what you could have celebrated.

Get back to work

John: Remember the vision God has given you and your team. Once again, tap into the mission you've been assigned to accomplish. Continue living out your core values. When people bolt, it may feel like it's the end of the world, but it's not. *A disgruntled member leaving your church doesn't change God's plan.* I suspect plenty of unchurched people live within a short distance of your building who would love you to be their pastor.

Plant and water. Dream and strategize. Execute and implement. Pour into those who remain. It's a losing strategy to spend more time with departing people than with those who are on board and rowing in the same direction as you. Focus like a laser on developing your leaders. You'll receive a disproportionate amount of great results in return.

You can't control who comes and goes. But you *can* offer a compelling experience for those who do come through your doors and stay. You *can* work toward creating a culture where they meet Jesus and experience true heart connection with other people. Work on what you can control. Trust God with what you can't.

When people bolt, take the high road. Avoid reacting; instead respond. Understand . . . grieve . . . say goodbye gracefully . . . then roll up your sleeves and get back to work. When people leave, remember the local church is more resilient than you imagine. Who knows? Your paths may cross again. And should that happen, you'll be glad you didn't erect an unscalable wall between you and the person(s) who left.

We've learned how to process when people arrive and when people leave. But are there ways to actually put the *good* in *goodbye?* Are there things we can do from the time of departure which create the potential of their return as better people? What does a leader do when those who've left decide to return? How do we receive them back?

Chapter seven outlines a strategy to welcome back into the church people who have left. Before you move on to the next chapter, take a few minutes to answer the questions below.

Questions to consider:
1. What are some practical ways you can bless people on their way out?
2. How can you grieve the loss of a person leaving without it consuming you?
3. Who can you talk to today about this?

7 | When People Come Back

If there is anything that will test your maturity in Christ as a servant leader, it's when people who leave very loudly, return (most of the time very quietly). People in this category tend to not mend relational fences broken by their immature behavior. At times they act as though they did nothing wrong.

It's been said, "Hurt people, hurt people" and in the case of leaving a church family there will be hurt. In this chapter, our goal is to help you . . . help them. Maybe they left for bad reasons. Maybe they said goodbye because it was time to leave. Maybe they moved on because they were legitimately hurt and needed time away.

Whatever the case, coming back into a community held together by trust and faith isn't as easy as sitting in your old seat and picking up where you left off. When trust and faith are broken, what does it look like to be restored? The following stories are all true. The hope in sharing them is not to commiserate, but to encourage you in loving the people who are hurt and very possibly hurting you, and if it's possible, to see them restored back into fellowship.

Family 1: Returning begins the day they leave

When an extremely influential family (comprising 25% of the total attendance and 45% of the monthly income in a small-town church of 100 people), decides they don't like the pastor any longer and want him to resign, the very worst in people can come out.

Such was the case with "Family 1." Not to give you the wrong impression, these were salt of the earth folks who loved God and people at a high level. If they had been cultists or control freaks, there wouldn't have been a problem.

These were simply good Christian people who had been raised under the same pastor their entire lives. After he retired and the new pastor was installed, they hoped the new guy would continue every cultural preference, every program, every song, style, and emphasis they previously enjoyed. Such was not the case. If it were doctrine being debated, resolution might have been possible. However, the division was caused more by culture and style than anything else.

The church operated the same way for decades, and now it was time to change just about everything in order to meet the world around it. When two points of view come from passionate, sincere people, all believing they're right, chances are the fur is about to fly.

After months of conversations and attempts to get the pastor to see they were correct, they decided the only course of action was to leave and let the church suffer in their absence. If the church failed, they could return at a time of their choosing and install another leader who would do what they sincerely believed was proper. What they didn't know was the day they left, was the day the pastor began to do whatever he could to get them back.

Some of you may be asking, "Get them back?" To which I say, yes, get them back. God is a God of reconciliation. I don't think He's nearly as passionate about cultural trends and church growth models as His children can be. One thing we all know: God is passionate about people caring for and loving each other, even if for a season, they are enemies.

> **God is passionate about people caring for and loving each other, even if for a season, they are enemies**

The next Sunday when the congregation met, everyone in the building, and most of the good folks in the small town, knew what had happened. Each one had formed an opinion about which side they were on.

Pews which had been filled by the faithful family for decades now sat empty. People whispered in the foyer to find out who was staying and who was leaving. Musicians, greeters, teachers, and friends were among the missing. People who were in the core of leadership and influence were now gone, angry, hurt and it seemed, never coming back.

The absences were obvious and unsettling. As the pastor began the sermon, he started the process of reconciliation with this family who wanted him to fail and leave. He asked the congregation to stand and make eye contact with him and said:

"We all know what's happened. Although differences of opinion exist even in this room today, before I open the Word of God, I ask everyone here to join me as we pray God's blessings on those who have left. We thank God for the incredible sacrifices they made for the gospel, this community, and us for decades."

This one prayer began a war of love fought for this family for the next ten years. First Corinthians 13 tells us "Love never fails." What it doesn't explain is, *although love never fails, it can take years to succeed.* Every time a barrage of words came toward the church in anger, hurt, or resentment, our congregation's response was to return words filled with love, compassion, and faith.

A fight takes at least two people. If one side stands their ground while at the same time turning their cheek, it's only a matter of time before most (not all) of those who would strike them see the error of their ways. If one side blesses those who curse them—if one side returns wrath with a gentle answer—and if one side is blessed with peace—it can't be long before the majority of those who stand on the side of war wonder if they didn't make a mistake.

Wrestling in the mud with pigs may seem emotionally satisfying at the moment, but remember, if you wrestle in the mud with pigs, you both get muddy and the pig likes it! The teaching of Jesus is clear: We are to bless, and when we do, we begin the process of healing for those who are hurt, including ourselves.

Family 2: Honesty is the beginning of reconciliation

After years of weekly meetings, Bob (not his real name) hadn't changed much, if at all. The one-hour sessions often went an hour or more over their allotted time. He was a good person who had seen God do great things but those things were all distant memories for him. In spite of his best efforts, he just wasn't able to get back to what he'd once had with God.

Hour after hour and week after week, Bob slowly slipped into despair and with his despair came the inevitable lusts and false idols the world so easily offers those who are desperate enough to indulge if just for one moment of pleasure. When it all fell apart, Bob did the unthinkable and confessed the affair he'd been hiding for months. His pastor listened to his broken heart as he confessed with great sincerity what he'd done and the emptiness his poor choices had created.

After prayer and Scripture reading, Bob asked the inevitable question, "What am I to do now?" His pastor told him the words he knew to be true, but Bob hoped for another way. "You have to now go and have the most difficult conversation of your life. You have to tell your wife and ask for forgiveness." He left after several hours of counsel, prayer, and Scripture, and went to have the conversation which in some ways would decide the rest of his life.

After a couple hours, Bob returned to see his pastor. The pastor put his day aside (again) for his friend and ushered him back to his private office so they could talk about how things had gone with his wife.

To his surprise, Bob seemed angry and began his thoughts with these words: "Well, I did what you told me to do and thanks for nothing! My wife is furious with me and threw me out of the house! I went to my mother's because I didn't know what to do, and she told me I should have never told my wife what happened! She said you gave me bad counsel!"

The stunned pastor sat and listened to this for several minutes as this man hurled accusations and insults at him out of his confusion and pain. After the storm began to subside, the pastor asked permission to ask a question. His question was at first baffling, but his point was soon to come. He simply said, "Bob, what color are your eyes?" Slightly dumbfounded by such a random question, Bob stuttered something about them being brown. The pastor leaned forward in his chair and said, "I thought they might be. Bob, you are so full of crap, I knew your eyes would be brown."

Bob sat shocked by these words from his otherwise gentle and kind pastor, and said nothing, but that didn't stop his pastor. For the next several minutes the pastor laid out for his friend the futility of the past several years of meeting, the ignored counsel, the waste of time and resources which could have been spent on someone who would have loved to have met with a pastor who cared for their soul. When he came to the end of his speech, he threw Bob out of his office, told him he was on his own, and not to return unless he was finally ready to deal with everything they had spoken about for the past several years.

We are not suggesting this as a normative practice, however, there are times when helping people may begin by hurting them with the truth. As you read this story, one of two things happened. You were either shocked by this pastor and the way he spoke to this hurting man or you laughed out loud thinking, "Man, I wish I would have done that a dozen times!"

The point of this true story is not to shock or entertain but to tell you what happened next. Because of the years of gentle loving care, this pastor had built a trust with Bob. Yes, he went away hurt and yes, it was his (Bob's) rock bottom. But, by facilitating this low point in his life, the pastor began the process of Bob's return to the church. Let me say it again: by throwing Bob out of the church, the pastor was beginning the process of bringing him back in as a healthy and restored soul.

When people leave the church, the reasons they left need to be dealt with before they come back. As pastors with more than forty-five years combined experience, we've observed many people who, after they return to church, are better for having gone through the process.

Those who leave loud and proud often return humble and teachable because of the pain of broken fellowship. Not everyone returns, but those who do have become some of the best people we have on the team. Many have taught us a great deal about the pain we caused them and have made us better servant leaders. Others came back realizing the grass was only greener because it was over a septic field, and now their expectations are more in line with reality.

No matter the excuse for someone leaving, being honest with them about the reason is always a good idea. Maybe you shouldn't ask them what color their eyes are, but maybe you should discuss the condition of their hearts.

Family 3: Letting people discover no perfect church exists

"Pastor, I'm leaving because this church isn't spiritual enough and I want to be where the fire is." The day Fred (not his real name) said this to me was an interesting day. What Fred didn't know was during the same time frame, I had been approached by others whose complaint was, "Pastor this church is too spiritual for me and I want something more comfortable for my family."

When Fred said these words, it didn't come as a surprise. He was just one of many families who were in the process of leaving for a variety of reasons. Their reasons ranged from the music volume, the room temperature, the gossip they'd heard, or even the reality that many of their friends now went to other churches. It just didn't "feel" like their church any more.

If you're a servant leader who is all in, this can be a trying time. It's a season you will most likely experience—if you stick around long enough. The truth is, people come and go, and nothing you do can change this reality. This is not meant to be discouraging. You have a choice to make when it happens. You can treat them like a deserter and order them stripped of rank, shot, and shunned, or you can treat them like the owner of Motel 6 and *"leave the light on for them."*

What I've experienced over the decades tells me the right thing to do. Even if Jesus hadn't spoken about this at great length and in precise detail, experience tells me: *loving people* is always the right thing to do in the long run. No other advice will bear more fruit.

If you let God love you enough, you'll start to love yourself like He does. If you love yourself like He does, you'll start to love people like He does, even if they are attempting to destroy your life's work. These are the seeds we are called to sow: *blessing not cursing; unity not division; truth not lies; peace not war; dying to yourself, not living selfishly.*

If you know what God has called you to do, do it. Turn the worship center's music volume up or down. Turn the thermostat up or down. Be a sincere expression of what you truly believe God wants you and the church you serve to be, and in the end, He will build His church.

Never forget, you are every man's servant but you only have One Master. Please Him, and let the chips fall where they may. If He's happy, then "Well done, good and faithful servant!" (Matthew 25:21). If He's not happy then . . . well . . . nothing you're doing really matters anyway. By letting people go, no matter their reason, and loving them through it all, you leave the door open for them to return as people who are wiser for having had you, and the love of God through you, in their lives.

Family 4: Not everyone will come back

"I'm upset with you, Pastor!" The angry voice on the other end of the phone was a good friend. Her use of the word "pastor" should have been my first clue something was wrong. Beth (not her real name) and her husband Scott (not his real name) served as key leaders in our church. We ate dinner with them, laughed with them, and their kids came over to our house to swim. If anyone had my back, it was Beth and Scott. I trusted them implicitly.

So you can understand why this call was quickly disorienting. Beth accused me of telling a story about her to a teacher at the elementary school where both her kids and our kids attended. It had to do with a situation the Bible would call a "disputable matter," (See Romans 14:1). Most people would label it a "gray area."

Beth took a very strong position on a debatable matter, and it affected things at school. A teacher questioned her stance, and asked Beth, "Why don't other people at your church have an issue with this?" For some reason, Beth thought *I* was one of those other people, and she convinced herself it was me who said something about it to the teacher.

When I replied, "Beth, that conversation never happened," it only made her angrier. She was convinced I was the culprit. The ensuing vocal barrage from Beth felt like hot knives thrust into my chest. I listened for ten minutes (not advisable) as the verbal punches continued. Whatever I said in response was rejected by Beth. I couldn't get her to believe my version of the event.

I hung up the phone. In shock, I stumbled home and let my wife know what just went down. How could someone I trusted, and who I thought trusted me, believe I would say something negative about her, and then lie to her about it? Beth and Scott remained at our church, but over the next few weeks it became clear an unscalable wall had been erected. My wife and I had dinner with them to try and smooth things over, but the damage was done—trust was gone. Relationships thrive on trust—they die without it.

Beth and Scott hung on for a couple of months, but soon let us know they would be leaving for another church. As much as I cared about them, I felt a degree of relief. I wished them the best, and unfortunately, that was the last time we ever talked.

Not everyone should come back. When a canyon of mistrust

exists, when you know you're being viewed under a legalistic microscope, when your every word and action is being scrutinized ... it might be time for a parting of ways.

Jim: It's been my experience that it can take up to ten years for a hurt person to reconcile and return. The clock is reset to square one if they hear you're talking badly about them. So, when it comes to processing the return of people who've left, remember these four things:

- Returning begins the day they leave.
- Honesty can be the beginning of reconciliation.
- Letting people go allows them to discover the grass isn't always greener at another church.
- Not everyone who leaves should come back.

In each scenario, commit to liberally seasoning your conversations with grace. Refuse to get drawn into the mud. Don't allow the bad behavior of others to dictate your behavior. Avoid the urge to retaliate. When those who've left return, your graciousness will be a bridge for them to walk back into church life.

Although this book is written primarily with the departure of lay people in mind, the vast majority of pastors have experienced the dynamics of a departing staff member. Chapter eight will briefly touch on the subject. Before you move to the next chapter, take a few minutes to read and answer the questions below.

Questions to consider:
1. How often have people who left your church decided to return at a later time?

2. How did you handle their return?
3. In this chapter, what is the most challenging principle for you to adopt? Why?
4. Who can you talk with to help you process your thoughts?

8 | When a Staff Member Leaves

The agitated voice of a shaken pastor rang in my ears. I (Jim) felt his pain, his concern, and his justifiable anger toward his former associate. While he vented, it dredged up memories of departing staff members from my team—some of them left of their own decision, others of mine—all of them hurt. Each departure created organizational waves I had to smooth out.

If you're a senior leader with a decade or more under your belt, you've probably heard or said things like:

> *"My associate pastor just announced his resignation, and told me he's starting a new church one mile down the road."*
> *"Pastor, we feel led to leave and take another position somewhere else."*
> *"I'm sorry, but after all our best efforts, the time for you to leave the staff has come."*
> *"I can't work here anymore!"*
> *"You're fired."*

Those are sentences which frequently followed many hours of agonizing effort, and often marked the end of a disappointing process which led to a staff member's departure.

Staff members don't have to be proven wrong to make their removal right

What is a leader to do when a staff member leaves or is dismissed? What's the best way to move forward? How do you know you're ready for departure scenarios?

Unfortunately, there is no best way to process the transition of a staff member. The wisest path is usually going to be determined on a case-by-case basis. (If you need assistance with a custom approach to an associate moving on, we are available to assist.) A staff member's departure is one time where "one-size-fits-all" can spell disaster. However, certain questions need to be asked in every case, and some principles are true in every situation. I suggest you consider each of the thoughts below carefully before taking any action.

Are you sure it's over?

Maybe, before you take the step of removing a staff member or accepting his or her resignation, a few actions to consider taking may prevent the transition. If the issue is burnout, they may be quitting prematurely. What they may need is rest, counseling, and a clear plan to get back in the game in a healthy way. If underperformance or even disloyalty is the problem, perhaps what they need is loving correction or a performance plan to get them back on track.

Remember, the staff members work for you, but you are *their* pastor. Your role in their lives doesn't change because of their performance level. People are replaceable but should never be expendable. We do real harm when we use up people and discard them.

Make sure it's over before you let someone go or accept his/her resignation. Do your best to make things work. At least then if it doesn't work out, you can look anyone in the eye (including yourself and God) and say, "I did everything I could to make things work. I have no regrets due to not trying hard enough."

Get facts straight and in writing if possible

The last thing you want in a departure situation is: "He said I did _____, but I say he did _____." If you have a board or elders, make sure everything is communicated to them in an honest and compassionate way. *Remember, your staff member doesn't have to be proven wrong to make their removal right.* If, (probably when), the stories of what really happened come out, and people's opinions begin to be shared, it's good to have specific information of who, what, when, and where, to firmly establish why removing this staff member was the right thing to do.

Never throw mud

". . . Love covers over a multitude of sins" (1 Peter 4:8). When we don't lovingly cover staff we've asked to leave, we harm the Body of Christ. I'm not suggesting you should be silent while someone destroys the church, but I am suggesting you should understand when a staff member is let go, hurt feelings are normal. Let's work to heal them as far as it depends on us.

You're the pastor. You're the one who is staying. Creating a culture where only "evil people" leave or are asked to leave is a mistake. It's taken me (Jim) up to ten years to reestablish relationships with people I've hurt, but as of this writing, everyone who has been released or left under stressful circumstances has been restored or is in the process. One negative or angry comment with them can start the reconciliation clock all over again.

Even if you've been completely wronged, mercy is the right thing. Honestly answer questions with statements like: "We agreed it was time," or "I'd love to reconcile with them and I'm praying for restoration." Remember, you don't have to make them wrong to be right. Take the high road and give God something to bless.

Fill in the blanks before the congregation does

I always announce in writing to the congregation any staff transitions so everyone gets the same news, at the same time, and in the same way. Of course, I first tell the staff, elders, deacons, and unpaid team leaders in the departing staff member's department.

This communication happens usually a week before the rest of the church hears the news. This allows time for them to digest it, ask questions, and be ready with answers to questions they will be asked. Filling in the blanks helps minimize "He said, she said" problems you won't hear about until they've gone around for a couple weeks unchecked.

Reassure the people affected by the change

Let them know your plans to fill the hole created by the departure, even if those plans are interim in nature. Assure those affected that you are committed to taking proper steps to make certain their ministry remains effective. Let them know your intentions about future staff or temporary promotions of unpaid leaders to interim leadership while you search for a more permanent solution.

Construct a kind but thoughtful severance package

Severance is an important consideration in staff departures. In cases where a series of paychecks remain to be written, consider allocating those checks over time, not in one lump sum. This could seem a little manipulative, but I believe it's both fair and wise depending on the circumstances.

I (Jim) let staff members know they will receive up to six weeks of pay, one week at a time, under specific, written terms they were originally hired to uphold. These terms might include integrity, honoring leadership, protecting the church, maintaining a good attitude and advocating for healthy relationships with the congregation. In short, I let them know we don't give money to individuals who would harm the church.

Consider an exit interview

This may seem a little masochistic in some cases, but I find people to be most honest when they have nothing to lose. If you want to be an excellent leader, an exit interview can be a growth exercise for you.

The hope is twofold: you will learn something to help you mature, and the departing staff member will feel heard. The interview also gives the person exiting an opportunity to vent their heart to *you*, and not to everyone else. If the idea of an exit interview freaks you out, perhaps someone else in leadership can conduct the interview, and relay a dispassionate version of it to you.

Manage your own heart and thoughts

I (John) cannot stress this final point enough. Formerly, I allowed the departure of a staff member to become a personal beatdown session (me beating myself down). Questions crashed like waves over my mind: "What's wrong with *me* that caused them to leave?" "How did I miss so badly on this hire?" "Will I ever get it right when it comes to adding staff?" "What kind of collateral damage will this departure create?" This negative internal interrogation often led me down a dark path.

What I didn't realize years ago is no leader bats a thousand percent when it comes to adding staff. None of us have perfected the art of hiring rock stars. No pastor has mastered the skill of leading a staff. I thought (foolishly) that staff members, like church members, were joined to me for as long as I led the church. I made the same mistake with them I had made with church members years ago. What I wish I knew thirty years ago is:

Staff members don't belong to me . . . they belong to God

More often than not, they grace our team for a season, and then, by their own choice or ours, they move on to another post. Can a staff member's longevity—or lack thereof—be a referendum on the quality of our leadership? Yes. Is it always? No. Healthy perspective comes when we understand and own our contribution (if any) to the departure, and allow the staff member to own his or her part.

When a staff departure gets difficult to sort through, double-time it to a mentor or wise friend. King Solomon wrote many years ago: "The purposes of a person's heart are deep waters, but one who has insight draws them out" (Proverbs 20:5). Feedback from a trusted source can help you think straighter when a staff member leaves.

Jim and I each have fired a few staff members, and some of them have left by their own decision. In every case, we felt some pain, anxiety, and doubt. We suspect you have walked a similar road. Working your way through the

Staff members don't belong to me . . . they belong to God

eight principles listed above during a departure are not easy, and won't necessarily lessen the pain, but it will likely reduce the amount of negative blowback surrounding the goodbye of a staff member.

In the next (and final) chapter, we'll leave you with a few exhortations. For those of you in a period of deep struggle, let these closing words bring inspiration, encouragement, and hope. If you are in a season of energizing momentum, let them shape your perspective.

Questions to consider
1. What process do you currently use to transition a staff member away from your team?
2. In what ways can you improve that current process?

9 | Final Words

At the very beginning of this book, we stated: Pastoring a church is not for the faint of heart. The role of pastor, especially senior or lead pastor, carries with it a weight of responsibility unknown to those who've never served in such a capacity. The best way we can describe the pressure is it feels like the lead vest the oral hygienist places on your chest prior to taking X-rays of your teeth. The underlying sense of responsibility never leaves, and it can wear down even the finest pastor.

When people arrive, if you're not careful, your chest can swell with pride. When they leave, it can feel like your chest is getting stomped on. We receive phone calls from pastors every week who ask: "Is pastoring worth the hassle?" We believe leading men and women is ultimately worth it, but requires understanding of, among other things, many of the ideas presented in this book. In order to put the *good* in *goodbye*, you'll need to operate with these five behaviors:

- Be certain of your call.
- Put God's people in their proper place. They belong to Him, not you.
- When folks arrive, it's probable their time with you is for a season.

- When members leave, be gracious and bless them upon their departure.
- When those who have left return, allow time for trust to be restored.

John: Serving as a lead pastor seems more complex today than it did thirty years ago. Society is more dysfunctional and less biblically literate. Competition for your people's time is at an all-time high. Culturally, things are changing faster than ever, and the Church is struggling to adapt. Expectations churchgoers have of their leaders remain high (and sometimes unrealistic).

Church members leave for legitimate reasons, or others for illegitimate ones—*yet I feel hopeful*. God is not wringing His hands in despair. He has a great game plan for your church in this generation; and He's willing to share it if you'll pause long enough to listen to Him, and *stay long enough* in one spot to implement what He says.

The painful sting of families leaving your church will probably never totally disappear. If you have a heart, you'll feel it when they bolt. But hopefully we've helped you look at their arrival and departure from a different perspective—perhaps from a healthier perspective—maybe even from God's perspective.

When people exit, you may think, "I'm next, I'm outta here, I can't take this anymore," and you begin fine-tuning your resumé. Resist such knee-jerk reactions. Like it or not, God allows the pressure of the role to squeeze you, and to push up hidden brokenness into your conscious awareness. People-pleasing, insecurity, and fear are exposed for the express purpose of God healing those fractured parts of your heart.

Before you even consider leaving, ask God: *"Have I learned in this assignment what You wanted me to learn?"* If no clear answer comes, and it seems He's put you in a holding pattern, perhaps there's something left for you to learn at your current post. Running at the first sign of trouble helps no one—including you.

> **No leader can stay healthy in relational purgatory**

If you're feeling overwhelmed, reach out for help. Every pastor needs a mentor, a coach, a friend. You can try to carry the pastoral burden alone—but why would you? In my opinion, no leader can stay healthy in relational purgatory. Being able to bounce ideas off others who will tell you the truth, having a team praying with you, and walking alongside people who make you laugh, just makes sense. This is especially true when you're figuring out how to process the comings and goings of people.

You've noticed the discussion questions at the end of each chapter. Many of them center around who you are talking to (or should be talking to) about processing the principles in this book.

Leadership health happens in community. The lone wolf pastor is a myth. You need multiple mentors speaking into your life, for the rest of your life—if you want to get and/or stay healthy. If you're operating alone, and don't know who to talk with, *Converge Coaching* would love the opportunity to come alongside and journey with you. We'd be honored if you reached out to us.

Finally, I (John) urge you to pay attention to your emotional health. No one will (or should) do that for you. Learn what recharges your emotional batteries. Schedule into your calendar regular times for rest, exercise, replenishing relationships, and laughter. Get enough sleep (6-9 hours per night). Inject a little boring into your life—God never called you to be on high alert 24/7. The healthier you are emotionally, the better prepared you'll be to process a church member's arrival or departure.

Pay attention to your emotional health

Jim and I deeply respect what you do for a living. We want you to win the war. But more importantly, we want you healthy.

Our wish for you includes a thriving marriage and family life. We want your kids to love Jesus. If you lose your ministry, you can still have a great life. If you lose your family, it will be much more difficult to have a great life, and you'll probably lose your ministry, at least for a season.

We want you to pastor for the long haul, and have fun at the same time. Our hope is the comings of people won't inflate you, and the goings of people won't deflate you.

Jim: When I was in Rome, I worked with an international church representing more than sixty nations in its congregation. It's one of the most fascinating groups of people on the planet. Africans, Asians, Latinos, Russians, Americans, refugees, and ambassadors fill this place several times a week to seek the Lord while living far from their home lands. Most of them have little in common with each other except their faith, which is more than enough.

On one of my days off a friend took me to the prison cell in the heart of the ancient city where Paul wrote his final epistle, 2 Timothy. As I sat in that dark, cold, wet place, I thought of how hopeless it must have felt.

Paul was no longer the great Apostle who wandered the known earth proclaiming Christ to entire regions. No longer was he being mistaken for one of the Greek gods because of the great power of Christ healing the sick and doing miracles. Now, he was the forsaken and for the most part forgotten prisoner who will soon be executed and disposed of as a nuisance to Rome.

His requests to his few remaining friends were simple: Remember me in prayer, carry on the work, bring me my extra cloak, and please remember my scrolls. This is a man saying goodbye to a world that hated him because he loved them.

I want you to see what's left of this man who has been beaten, stoned, imprisoned, shipwrecked, abandoned, and betrayed (See 2 Corinthians 11:25). What's left is his faith *in* and trust *for* Jesus. Everything and just about everyone else is gone. His greatest statement in my opinion was this, "I have fought the good fight, I have finished the race, I have kept the faith" (2 Timothy 4:7).

The greatest test of your ministry (and your life) will not be measured in numbers but by your fidelity when things get hard. As a follower of Christ, quitting is a luxury you can no longer afford. I'm not saying there is never a time to go somewhere else or do something else. What I'm saying is there is no quitting, there is only finishing.

Our prayer for you is: To finish the work God sent you to accomplish by His grace and power, and to hear at the end of your time on earth, "Well done, good and faithful servant! You have been faithful in a few things; I will put you in charge of many things. Come and share your master's happiness!" (Matthew 25:21).

We are rooting and praying for you!

John and Jim

The End

About the Author: John

John Opalewski graduated from Oral Roberts University and served as a pastor for 16 years. He is a certified Coach with Natural Church Development (NCD). He has served as an associate pastor, campus pastor, and lead pastor. For 20 years, John also worked in the Information Technology industry.

John's experience as a leader in both the church and business arenas has made him a sought-after international speaker, consultant, and mentor. John and his wife, Laura, founded Converge Coaching, LLC in 2012 to help leaders be effective in their roles while maintaining health in their personal lives.

Additional books available for purchase through John's website: www.convergecoach.com

eBook platforms also available:
Amazon Kindle
Barnes & Noble (Nook)
iBookstore
Sony
Kobo
Copia
Gardners
Baker & Taylor
eBookPie

Contact and Ordering Information

Bulk discounts available

For more information about other resources and services available through Converge Coaching, LLC, please visit our website: www.convergecoach.com

To contact John email him at: john@convergecoach.com

About the Author: Jim

Jim Wiegand is an ordained minister and along with his wife, Dena, has pastored The Freedom Center in Fenton Michigan for the past 22 years. During his tenure, TFC has planted or parented 5 churches in the U.S. Specializing in leadership development, the staff of TFC has come entirely from within the congregation, with longevity and family health as the focus.

Jim is also the author of *Why is Greater than What: Discovering Your Passion* and is a sought-after speaker, teacher, and trainer. *Why is Greater than What* is available in paperback or e-book at 199seconds.com.

Additional Resources from Converge Coaching

Unshakable You
5 Choices of Emotionally Healthy People
John Opalewski

Emotional health can be elusive. We often run our lives on fumes, dangling on the edge of burnout or depression. Difficult relationships, overcommitted schedules, traumatic events, or the gnawing sense we're unlovable, drain our energy.

What can you do? If you're burnt out or depressed, how do you get healthy? If you're healthy, how do you stay that way? You start by making five choices. *Unshakable You: 5 Choices of Emotionally Healthy People*, introduces key behaviors which move a depressed person toward recovery, and keep an emotionally fit person well.

Pick up a copy today at www.convergecoach.com
E-book available on iPad, Kindle, Nook, Kobo, Copia and many other platforms

**Take Charge of Your Mental
& Emotional Health**
John Opalewski

Learn how to take ownership of your mental and emotional health. This four-part series—available in DVD and CD formats—offers practical help and hope to those suffering with depression. It equips emotionally healthy people to stay well-adjusted, while effectively helping those in depression's grip.

Pick up a copy today at www.convergecoach.com

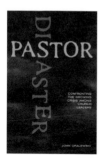

Pastor Disaster
Confronting the Growing Crisis
among Church Leaders
John Opalewski

Pastoring a church can be hazardous to a leader's health. Difficult people, dysfunctional families, unrealistic expectations, and spiritual warfare present challenges to a pastor's longevity and health. More than 1,000 pastors leave the ministry every month due to burnout, contention in their church, or moral failure. Their exodus has contributed to the decline of the Church's impact on Western culture.

The question is . . . what can we do? How can leaders lead longer and better? This practical guide, written for pastors, leaders, and churchgoers, identifies the real problems behind the current leadership crisis. It provides workable solutions to strengthen leaders and help the Church re-establish its influence.

Pick up a copy today at www.convergecoach.com
E-book available on iPad, Kindle, Nook, Kobo, Copia and many other platforms